SURVIVOR PSYCHOLOGY

The Dark Side of a
Mental Health Mission

KINGMAN

SUSAN SMITH

Upton
B O O K S

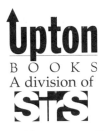

Upton
B O O K S
A division of

SIRS

Social Issues Resources Series, Inc.
P.O. Box 2348
Boca Raton, FL 33427
Copyright © 1995 by SIRS, Inc.
Limited Edition

Library of Congress Cataloging-in-Publication Data

Smith, Susan, 1953-
    Survivor psychology: the dark side of a mental health mission /
Susan Smith
        p.   cm.
    Includes bibliographical references and index.
    ISBN 0-89777-138-9 : $14.95
    1. False memory syndrome. 2. Repression (Psychology).
3. Memory. 4. Victims. 5. Psychiatric ethics. I. Title.
RC455. 2. F35S64 1995   94-42575
616.89'14—dc20   CIP

Cover design by Michelle McCulloch

SURVIVOR PSYCHOLOGY

TABLE OF CONTENTS

Chapter One

Introduction to the Issues

*Orthodox medicine has not found
an answer to your complaint.
However, luckily for you,
I happen to be a quack.*

—Richter cartoon caption

Some of today's counselors and psychotherapists are promoting dangerous trends: most notably, beliefs presented as science, and fanaticism justified by excessive pandering to the notion of "erring on the side of the victim." These trends, in tandem with therapeutic social-reform and recovery movements, have contributed to a climate in which an ideological therapy system, known as "survivor therapy," has developed and flourished. Those promoting this brand of therapy often belong to a new category of self-proclaimed "experts," who specialize in identifying and treating repressed memories of sexual abuse.

To claim expertise in "repressed memories" is a contradiction in terms. Even truly qualified and recognized social scientists and academicians—those with decades of research and scientific publications on memory to their credit—do not claim expertise in repression or repressed memories. Though memory repression is thought to be a viable theory by some, there is still no relevant research to support the validity of the concept. Those qualified and informed enough to be conservative about memory repression and memory processes do agree on one major point: Since very little is actually known about repression and memory processes, the theories and methods used, even in responsible therapy systems, are to be cautiously applied, and according to many, preferably not used at all.

Is it merely coincidental that while new categories of "mental illnesses," "addictions," and "disorders" continue to multiply, and the ways in which victimization is defined expand, that the number of therapists continues to rise? In addition to becoming a nation in which people define themselves as victims with the slightest provocation, many willingly surrender their psychological integrity to anyone with the audacity to claim special abilities and a desire to "heal" others of their numerous dysfunctions. Abdicating both control and responsibility is endemic to this trend. Under the influence of a therapist, or simply due to over-exposure to the pervasive therapeutic thinking in the culture, many become all too willing to search for reasons to identify with victim status. This should not be surprising, since the therapeutic emphasis has shifted from resolving past traumas, completing unfinished business and making adjustments, to *finding out* about presumably repressed memories of trauma and *connecting* present difficulties with numerous items that are said to be *symptoms* of repressed traumatic memories.

George Santayana (1863-1952) aptly described how idealism evolves into fanaticism when he said, "Fanaticism consists of redoubling your effort when you have forgotten your aim." Santayana could have been describing the radical ideology associated with the survivor-therapy movement, the perpetuation of which has become more important than the well-being of clients, both individually and collectively.

Survivor Psychology: The Dark Side of a Mental Health Mission will explain the origins, foundations and theories that have contributed to the growth and development of a mental-health movement that has evolved into a moral crusade. The crusade has now become a cause—not a cure—of victim syndromes, social deviance and persecution. As much as we know about violence in the family, violence in society and violence against women and children, there is an insidious, bloodless violence most people know very little about—the violence done in the name of psychotherapy.

In the past several years, thousands of parents have been

4

accused of everything from "emotional incest" to cannibalism, infanticide, rape, serial murder and satanic ritual abuse. In trying to be supportive, sometimes siblings and other family members become enmeshed in the same therapeutic system that entrapped a family member, and end up suspecting or coming to believe they were also abused as children—and they had never remembered or realized it before going to therapy.

Many parents and other family members have progressed through the fairly predictable stages of grief—denial, anger, bargaining and an uneasy acceptance—without the final stage of resolution. For many broken families there can be no resolution until the family is restored and the accusations recanted.

Many parents would welcome their adult child or children home and never speak of the devastating accusations. Others are not sure this is possible or healthy for anyone involved. And, after all, it was the pursuit of "recovery" or reputedly "healthy" ways of living and open communication that set most of their children on the course that caused their estrangement from the family, and propelled them into a cultish enmeshment with therapy, recovery and self-help systems. If the processes of healing through therapy— "memory work" and identification with pathological labels and victim syndromes—are so healthy and healing, why do we have so many new "diseases," victims of therapeutic abuse and survivor syndromes? Many of these alleged survivors claim they had absolutely no awareness of any trauma or abuse until they sought therapy, became involved in recovery groups or found therapists who claimed they were experts in memory retrieval and in recognizing "repressed sexual abuse issues."

The Dawning of Disease Labels
The behavioral pathology craze of the 1980s, in which

everything from excessive shopping to incest became a 12-step treatable "disease," has evolved into a complete system of thought, language, treatment propaganda and aggressive therapeutic modalities that is identified herein as "survivor psychology."

The phrase "recovery culture" generally refers to the 12-step groups. These groups have been a primary vehicle for the conceptualization and spread of survivor psychology. Moreover, recent developments fomenting within some churches may soon displace 12-step programs and other pedestrian psychology systems in the invention, marketing and "treatment" of imaginary or fanciful diseases or syndromes. Some radical new "Christian counseling" programs are far more slick, ideologically overinvested and organized than 12-step recovery culture groups. These programs have adopted recovery culture language and theory, but have also resurrected a form of medieval psychology, with an aggressive emphasis on myths and superstitions leading to the escalation of reports involving satanic ritual abuse (SRA).

Many self-proclaimed experts in memory recovery and repressed memory syndromes have built their theories and treatment plans on contemporary urban legends and pseudoscience. Confabulation occurs under different circumstances, including organic brain disorders. But in general, confabulation means to fill in memory blanks with plausible-sounding details. Emotionally loaded terminology and an internally consistent system of "survivor logic" are used to justify the aggressive and invasive treatment practices by which many seeking help are getting worse.

The "body memory" notion is one of those pseudoscientific beliefs that survivor psychologists use to support their system of therapy and ideology. It is generally believed that the body memory notion is a recent "discovery" brought about through trauma-resolution therapy and various forms of body work. The notion is not new, and has been used in several fringe and quack therapy systems since the 1950s.

There are some legitimate uses of body work that may facilitate physical and emotional trauma resolution. The careful and responsible work of many therapists is in danger of being dismissed because of aggressive applications of techniques used to bring about traumatic abreactions that are labeled body memories. The body-memory theory may be the most dangerous and persuasive notion promoted by the survivor movement.

It is almost heretical to criticize the recovery movement or the survivor movement. Protecting the children, stopping the cycle of child abuse and the cycle of violence, learning to be more loving and respectful of ourselves, our children and others, and becoming genuine, honest, responsible human beings are admirable and noble aspirations. But good intentions do not always produce good results. The cycle of violence is being perpetuated in new and unusual ways. Some adults suffer the primary abuse at the hands of aggressive therapists and some children suffer primary victimization by the child protective establishment.

A Toxic "Solution" to the Human Condition

The mental health and emotional hygiene missionaries seem to think they have done the impossible. They have completely exposed the mysteries of human nature and answered all the big questions that have plagued humanity for centuries. Why are people the way they are? Why do people commit acts of violence or blindly follow the crowd? Why are people stubbornly self-destructive and sometimes just plain stupid? Why do we have wars, crime, addiction and social problems? Why do we have cruelty, prejudice and fanaticism? To these timeless questions, the recovery culture has settled on its own unambiguous answer: *The family is a pathological system that is unconsciously organized around the abandonment and soul-murder of children.* John Bradshaw has been both credited and reviled for practically divining or discovering this ideology, but the major ideas come from the work of Swiss psychoanalyst Alice Miller.

In other words, bad parenting is the cause of the world's problems. According to recovery culture theory, we have all been abandoned by our parents, and this abandonment has caused an inner self-rupture that is called "shame-binding." In *Bradshaw On: The Family,* John Bradshaw states the basic premise of "recovery":

> The crisis is far worse than anyone knows because the adults who parent their children were also abandoned and are separated from their own true inner selves. The adults who parent are covering up their shame-based inner selves. So the crisis is not just about how we raise our children; it's about a hundred million people who look like adults, talk and dress like adults, but are actually adult children. These adult children run our schools, our churches and our government. They also create our families. This book is about the crisis in the family today—*the crisis of adult children raising children who will become adult children.*

Bradshaw leads up to the conclusion that Nazism, Jonestown and Mylai are the consequences of "insidious family rules" that lead to obedience without critical judgment and inner freedom. His conclusions are seductively simple and emotionally appealing. His solutions sound convincing and well-intentioned, but there is a catch. In order to achieve the "healing" promised by recovery and survivor-psychology promoters, you must accept the premises of the systems, which are by no means simple, innocuous or any more liberating than any other cult psychology system.

The mindless submission carefully cultivated in the recovery culture can be easily exploited. When a person who uncritically accepts these premises encounters ideologically overinvested therapists, he or she may be inclined to accept seductive and simple solutions attached to still further conditions of surrender and mindlessness. Surrender and mindlessness, or dissolution of ego boundaries and intellectual processes for immediate experience, are not inherently undesirable states of being. It is when these conditions are cultivated under false pretenses, for the purposes of control and indoctrination, that they are dangerous.

Questionable Therapies, Incredible Claims

Resolution and acceptance are natural processes that occur for people who make the transition from youthful self-absorption to greater self-actualization—or at least a healthy acceptance of human limitations. But something has happened to many baby boomers on the way to adulthood. The therapeutic culture may have helped some individuals in the maturation and acceptance process. But others have clearly been impeded.

It is practically inevitable that relationships with parents, family members or childhood caretakers are the longest-running and most deeply felt relationships most people ever have. The so-called "taboos" that prevent adults from expressing anger against parents have been broken by the latest mental and emotional health fad known as "recovery." Millions of adults have been caught up in a therapeutic ideology that is organized around the notions that "you must get worse before you get better," "you're only as sick as your secrets," "you can't heal what you can't feel," and the "only way out is through."

In a limited sense, these slogans have always contained grains of truth. It is also true that children have traditionally suffered because adults were supposed to be respected and obeyed, whether they had the wisdom to exercise authority responsibly or not. It is part of the process of maturation to confront taboos, but it is also important to maintain some degree of objectivity about what this confrontation can accomplish.

The spread of therapeutic ideologies is complicated by a cultural bias that is supportive of any program, group or therapist claiming to be doing good by dealing with the dirty business that no one else presumably wants to deal with or to which no effective solution has been found. The most glaring example of this is alcohol abuse and the AA program. The public complacency regarding AA infiltration into all our social institutions has nothing to do with the proven effectiveness of recovery through the AA philosophy. Participation in the AA religion is often court-ordered because it costs nothing and offers "the last chance" for "hopeless addicts." It is assumed that addicts should be grateful for the philosophical and religious conversion cure offered by AA, which will "work if they work it."

The intentions certainly seem admirable, but the assumption that good intentions invariably produce good results has contributed to the erosion of boundaries between law, religion, academia, mental health and addictions treatment. Meanwhile, survivor psychologists are spinning new ideologies or embellishing old theories to counter the mounting criticisms of their unscientific methods and outlandish beliefs. Many of them scoff at the word "scientific" and claim that the mysteries of the mind and emotions are beyond science. And it is precisely because human subjective reality cannot be easily studied or scientifically dissected that great care must be taken with subjective issues. It is true that great emotional and psychological risks must be taken in life if the mature potential for creative expression and emotional depth is to be reached. But some survivor psychologists may have forgotten that the journey is an inner process leading to greater independence, love, understanding, freedom and tolerance. Inner work was never intended to be a psychodrama acted out upon others, or a process of retaliation to achieve healing.

The new ideology of survivor psychology is that revenge is healthy. Incest-related publications encourage readers to seek financial compensation for past child abuse. But there are no clear definitions of child abuse or sexual abuse in survivor psychology. And even worse, having no memories of child abuse is supposed to indicate really horrible repressed memories. Now parents are being sued and rejected for what adult children don't remember, as well as for what they "come to believe" or dig up in the process of aggressive therapies.

Sexual exploitation of children is a crime and should be treated as such, but charges of pedophilia are serious and should not be made frivolously, or redefined to take in notions of psychic sexual abuse like "covert incest" and "emotional incest." Communication occurs on the unseen or psychic level at all times, but it is not possible to quantify or evaluate the content of these communications for the purposes of accusing or convicting people of sexual crimes or child abuse.

The recent belief that all past abuse, real or created in the therapeutic process, must be avenged and compensated financially may soon reveal itself to be ineffective as a method of emotional healing. In fact, it may cause people to compensate for their actions by identifying even more profoundly with victim status and increase a collective and overdeveloped sense of entitlement that has already done immense damage in this society.

When family members and critics are made the "enemy" by counseling and mental health ideologies, we have a situation where no one wins, and, ultimately, everyone loses. The enemies are not education, social activism, criticism, research, respect for the unknown, tolerance for ambiguity and science. The enemies are ideology, elitism and fanaticism.

The issues in question are not a matter of believing or discounting personal and individual testimonials in which clients claim therapists "saved their lives" by unearthing repressed memories or integrating their multiple personalities. What is at stake here are the professional ethics of the mental health field and the lives of primary and secondary victims of therapeutic abuse. Primary victims are those enmeshed in aggressive therapy systems. Secondary victims are the family members impacted by false accusations or the psychological deterioration that often accompanies memory recovery therapy. "Retractors"—individuals who have since renounced the memories they had "unearthed" in therapy—have reported therapy costs often exceeding several hundred thousand dollars. Their stories epitomize the disintegration that can occur with aggressive therapies.

People in need put their trust in professionals who have earned the title of "doctor." The terms "psychologist," "psychoanalyst" and "counselor," though technically distinct, may be practically synonymous with the title of doctor to people outside of the mental health field. These titles imply ethical standards, social responsibility, special knowledge, education, research and *science*. Consequently, mental health practitioners, with and without degrees, are considered authorities by clients. Clients are not generally aware that most of the official-sounding terminology some therapists and analysts use are merely metaphorical notions and sometimes outright fabrications that have no basis in research.

When therapists start talking about "cellular memories" or "body memories" and "state-dependent learning," the client often takes these notions as empirical truth when they are no more than theories, beliefs and misconceptions. Survivor psychologists are fond of attributing their opinions to "clinical experience" when they deal with clients and write pop survivor books. In fact, they are less like clinicians than they are like fortune tellers, high-powered salespeople, con artists, self-proclaimed psychics and faith healers.

The spread of survivor psychology is not limited to bad or untrained therapists. And though critics of survivor therapy have noted that practically anyone can call him or herself a "psychotherapist," it may be an even worse problem when people with credentials and degrees peddle urban legends and irresponsible and hysterical theories. Mental health practitioners should not hide behind the respectable facade of professionalism while selling philosophical snake oil and practicing various forms of quackery. *Survivor Psychology* may also help explain how otherwise intelligent people become entrapped in the therapeutic systems that seem so obviously manipulative to outsiders or to family members who become the secondary victims of invasive and aggressive therapy systems.

This book is written with the hope that mental health professionals will read it through and not just assume it is an exercise in therapist bashing. There are still many responsible therapists to whom the health and well-being of clients, maintaining professional integrity, seeking the truth and preserving the hard-earned respect accorded to the mental health profession, are primary concerns. Perhaps establishing points of agreement, and then moving from a position of common goals will be the best starting place from which to attempt to work out resolutions to these issues.

Chapter Two

A Sociological Context for the Evolution of Survivor Psychology

*Markets as well as mobs respond
to human emotions; markets as
well as mobs can be inflamed
to their own destruction.*

—Owen D. Young

The survivor therapy phenomenon is a consequence of our newly developed cultural inability to take stands on issues of personal responsibility. The initial stages of this social evolution evolved out of long-awaited and much needed changes in the ways in which women, children and minorities have been treated. Exposing inhumanity and social inequity has been enlightening and will continue to be essential to social change. Yet there are times when it seems that the benefits are outweighed by the negative consequences. The development of the system of survivor psychology is one of those consequences.

This is the first time in history that thousands of adults are claiming that they are "recovering memories" of abuse that had been totally repressed for decades. The survivors of the Holocaust, both children and adults, knew they were survivors and were able to identify war criminals decades later. The Canadian orphans raised by the nuns of St. Julienne in the 1940s and 1950s were put in straitjackets, tied to metal beds, shocked and allegedly beaten and raped. Though mentally normal, they were declared retarded in order to collect extra support from the Canadian welfare system. The orphans knew they had been abused and some are now seeking justice. Many survivors of traumatic childhoods or other terrible tragedies are lucky if they can make it a week and not think about what happened to them or others.

Other ways of dealing with trauma, which are often labeled repression, may include refusing to think about the trauma, suppressing thoughts about the trauma until it is considered essentially "forgotten," and occasional traumatic amnesia that often involves head wounds or a state of shock occurring after an accident or a deep emotional trauma. However, total amnesia afflicting a large portion of an entire generation is extremely unlikely.

Freud used the term repression to describe the psychological tendency to screen out or deny socially unacceptable impulses or taboo thoughts. Neither Freud nor his ideological descendants used repression to mean wholesale amnesia over months or years of actual events. So how is it that repression has assumed mythical proportions? Why would the baby boom generation be the first generation in history to proclaim themselves victims of repressed memory syndromes on a large scale? Were adults becoming progressively more pathological during our formative years?

Did the 12-step recovery culture and "The Course in Miracles" and all the other pop psychology and mental health missionaries really come along just in time to save the children from their "toxic parents," and society from moral decay presumably caused by toxic parenting? Is our culture truly spiritually and morally bankrupt, as the mental health missionaries claim it is—or will be without their "programs," therapeutic ideologies, interventions and in-patient treatment?

The truth is that addiction, child abuse and family violence are, and have been, present in most societies. Taking this simple fact into consideration, and replacing nostalgic cultural mythologies about the "good old days" for a more historically accurate account, a different view emerges. Historically, the evidence is overwhelming that human beings have been fascinated by altered states of consciousness, or utilized plant chemicals for specific purposes. Various medicinal, narcotic, stimulating and psychoactive plants have been consumed since the Stone Age.

In the early 19th century, per capita alcohol consumption was almost three times higher than it is today. An epidemic of cocaine and opium addiction swept the United States during the late 19th century. The drugs were cheap, legal and dispensed in large quantities by pharmacists. The rich and middle class often became addicted because of too much money, too much time and sheer availability. Child labor laws were not enacted until the 1920s. In the early 1900s children made up 23 percent of the work force in the textile factories of major cities like Chicago, New York and Boston. Children as young as seven or eight worked 12-hour shifts and slept on piles of rags in the factories.

The nuclear family is primarily a media invention spawned in the wake of World War II. The idealized image of homemaking was part of the ad campaign to drive women out of the work force and into a romanticized home life, complete with all the modern labor-saving devices signifying the ease of the impending "Space Age" that never quite arrived. As Stephanie Coontz, author of *The Way We Never Were: American Families and the Nostalgia Trap*, says, "Our most powerful visions of traditional families derive from images that are still delivered to our homes in countless reruns of 1950s television sitcoms." Coontz argues that contemporary mythmaking about the "golden age" of the family has fueled a sense of guilt and "rage and betrayal" over a failure to achieve the illusory dream. Judging from the survivor phenomenon, this is particularly pronounced among the boomers, the first generation to be reared on television and contemporary media mythology. It would be foolish to ignore the impact and power of television in shaping attitudes and consensus reality in contemporary society. Television has established itself as an extremely potent sales medium as well as an instrument of socialization. It is also the primary vehicle by which many people experience the world and formulate opinions. As such, television is the ideal tool for coercion. Terence McKenna, author of *Food of the Gods,* elaborates:

> Control of content, uniformity of content, repeatability
> of content make it inevitably a tool of coercion, brain-
> washing, and manipulation. Television induces a trance
> state in the viewer that is the necessary precondition
> for brainwashing.

The terms coercion, manipulation or brainwashing do not imply that the person is completely unconscious, defenseless or unaware. These terms actually refer to the use of influence and indoctrination tactics, and reliance upon pseudoscientific notions, "factoids" and thinly veiled political ideologies. When combined with hypnosis, trance work, age regression, leading lines of questioning, selective reinforcement of expected or desired responses and "rage work," such techniques may shape attitudes and bombard the client with cues, rewards and reinforcement for behaviors that "validate" the suspected diagnosis of repressed memories.

Many therapists deny using formal hypnosis, yet most of the modalities already mentioned are inherently hypnotic. Apparently, inadvertent hypnosis and suggestibility are not understood by many mental health practitioners. Social psychologist Richard Ofshe says that when leading lines of questioning are pursued while a client is in a highly suggestible state, even if the altered state has been inadvertently or unintentionally induced, it becomes the most dangerous and coercive means of manipulating suggestibility.

Aggressively penetrating clients' defense mechanisms by formal and informal hypnosis, compliance techniques, group and peer pressure, and other tactics of influence, have become common treatment modalities. Survivor and recovery psychologists claim that it is their role to "take patients on a guided trip back into the hell of their childhoods," and "grief work" or "original pain work" is essential to their notions of the process of healing. While being aware of your feelings is a legitimate goal of therapy, there is absolutely no proof that stripping people of their emotional and intellectual survival skills is inherently therapeutic.

The baby boom generation is largely comprised of those who enjoyed extended and fairly privileged childhoods. This doesn't mean everyone was economically privileged, but even poor families in the 1950s received far more resources than current government programs provide. Subsidy programs such as the GI Bill and government-underwritten loans enabled more people to attend college or buy a home. The general levels of prosperity and the promotion of the American Dream created high expectations that have been thwarted by numerous social, global, environmental and economic developments. The interactive effects of these stressors, the short-sightedness cultivated by the romanticism of the American Dream, and the ideals of therapy, may have created a predisposition to recovery culture psychology, particularly when disappointments become evident in mid-life. It is a psychological tendency to sometimes revise personal history, often with the individual casting him or herself in the best possible light. When past failures are attributed to the wrongdoings of others, personal responsibility is avoided or denied.

From Psychiatry to Sidewalk
Psychology and Survivor Therapy

The shift from diagnostic or "pathology-oriented" thinking to therapeutic thinking gained acceptance in the 1960s and 1970s. During these two decades the willingness to enter therapy or self-exposure groups came to be viewed as a sign of healthy adjustment. Avoiding therapy or groups was a sign of neurosis or unhealthy inhibitions. Therapeutic thinking had barely gained social acceptance when the 12-step recovery culture began to proliferate in the urban underground. Now the two have merged. The diagnostic language of psychiatry has trickled down into mainstream culture through the sidewalk psychology underground. Confessional orgies, self-diagnosis sessions and "wounded healers" selling crypto-pornographic tales of sex and violence are standard TV talk show fare. Now everyone is "sick" but no one is responsible. Now our national slogan and talk show theme is "you're only as sick as your secrets." No one is responsible for their "diseases" (which used to be behaviors), but everyone is responsible *for his or her own recovery.*

In itself, therapeutic thinking may not be dangerous. But literally interpreting "inner work" and reframing the past in pathological terms may do more harm than good. The modern aggressive analytic process of constructing a therapeutically correct narrative truth seems to create drama and inflict trauma. Lynn Gondolf, a constructed memory retractor, comments: "Repressed memories of sexual abuse and satanic abuse are the favorites among therapists. All the elements of a good soap opera are there—sex, drama and money."

. The notion that "emotional openness" was healthier than being "closed off" or reserved continued to gain acceptance until negative self-disclosure became a media industry. A publishing empire was built on drunkalogues, shamealogues and confessions of every nature, followed by 12-step testimonials or high praise for the benefits of therapy. Formerly rare conditions, such as Multiple Personality Disorder (MPD) and Post Traumatic Stress Disorder (PTSD) are now diagnosed and discussed regularly, usually with little or no regard for accuracy.

Many survivor psychology theories have emerged through 12-step, adult-child and dysfunctional family oriented theorists. By the mid 1980s these theories became generalized and applied to 100 percent of the population by virtue of two criteria: Being raised in a family, which was reframed by recovery culture theorists to be the toxic vehicle for transmitting dysfunctionality; and being a member of society, which has been denounced as nothing more than an "addictive process system" by recovery writers such as Anne Wilson Schaef.

By the late 1980s it was no longer necessary to have specific problems pertaining to alcohol or other drugs within the family to be an "adult child." One only had to be born to become "dysfunctional."

The Lockout on Open Debate

As our culture became increasingly desensitized to pathological labeling and developed an excessive reliance on the world views of amateur family systems theorists, the autobiographies and interviews of famous or public personalities became riddled with recovery culture jargon. Gloria Steinem's *Revolution from Within* and Patty Davis's *The Way I See It* are minor studies in the most provincial recovery culture theories.

Subjective experience is direct experience, and honest communication involving emotions and experiences is not at issue here. The issue is the aggravating and obviously manipulative practice of using "I messages" as smokescreens for delivering mini-sermons. There is a difference between honest communication and covert 12-stepping, counseling or preaching. In discussion, "what works for me" becomes a means to shut down dialogue and abort interaction. If you say "I think," you're "intellectualizing" and "not taking responsibility" for, or "owning," your feelings.

The eerie social condition of continual therapy creates an impotent political and educational environment. For example, in my own experience as a graduate student, the class discussions were nearly devoid of critical thinking and debate. Therapeutic talking has been so well integrated into the culture and the academic environment that debates and discussions were often derailed by some querulous request that we please limit our comments to "I messages." I was asked to "rephrase" my concerns about issues in society and those apparent in the counseling curriculum. Communication is turned into a semantic shuffle and a matter of sentence structure. Instead of saying, "I'm concerned about some of the course material in the counseling curriculum," I'd be asked to "rephrase" and say, "I concern myself over the course material," and then the course material was no longer the issue—why I chose to be concerned becomes the issue. The issue was then shifted from the accuracy of claims made in recovery books, assumptions being promoted by educators (and largely agreed upon among students), to my problem. Either I was not "in recovery," thus could not possibly understand the issues, or I was "in denial" and not "in touch with my feelings."

Questioning the efficacy of therapeutic modalities, examining the methods used, reassessing assumptions and comparing results and consequences of various procedures and philosophies, is of great importance in the therapeutic process.

The questions are of paramount importance. Both primary and secondary victims of therapeutic abuse are asking questions. Now the very same movements that instigated the questions about entrenched social assumptions and social systems are now the most aggressively critical of those analyzing current social systems and questioning the wisdom of exaggeration and fabrication. The chapter to follow addresses some of the most common criticisms and questions regarding survivor therapy, survivor psychology, and social developments arising from this phenomenon.

24

Chapter Three

Repressed Memories and Survivor Psychology: Questions, Criticisms and Answers

One who would distinguish the true from the false must have an adequate idea of what is true and false.

—Baruch Spinoza

In 1992 I completed a research project involving 38 therapists claiming to specialize in repressed memories, sexual abuse and incest issues. Since then, I have often been asked to discuss the results and talk about the repressed memory and survivor phenomenon. The sequences to follow deal with some of the most common issues, but by no means cover them all. These are actual questions, observations and criticisms as they have been posed to me during talks, personal communications and other encounters.

How would you define survivor psychology?

Survivor psychology is a system of beliefs, internal logic and therapeutic techniques. The system borrows liberally from Freudian theories and procedures, various learning theories, family systems theories, metaphysics, 12-step fundamentalism, religious fundamentalism (including demonology), and pseudoscientific or even entirely bogus physiological and psychological theories. It is a literalistic, simplistic meld of retrograde mind-cure philosophies, reinforced by Freudian notions and various therapeutic techniques, which are often considered "fringe modalities" by critics of radical or unconventional therapies. These techniques include "relaxation" techniques, guided imagery, age regression, directive and interpretive psychodramas, non-dominant handwriting, trance writing, visualization, group processes, art therapy, and play therapy.

What is repressed memory syndrome?

Repressed memory syndrome refers to the vast number of syndromes, psychiatric disorders, addictive disorders, medical diseases and emotional disturbances purportedly caused by traumatic memories for which the conscious mind has created barriers and rendered unavailable to awareness. There is no scientific evidence that supports the theory of repressed memory syndromes as presented by the survivor psychology movement.

It is important to stress that critical appraisal and research into these issues does not suggest that memories are never repressed, or that true traumatic memories might not sometimes surface in a responsible therapeutic relationship. However, what we are dealing with in survivor psychology is largely the *belief* in repressed memory syndromes. Beliefs can create expectations which can influence the direction of interaction, and ultimately, the outcome of therapy.

I heard you say that survivor psychology is less like a system of therapy, and more like a system of influence, persuasion and sales psychology. Can you explain that a little more?

It is often assumed that the number of people involved in a phenomenon or believing in an idea determines the basic truth inherent in the belief or phenomenon. The survivor psychology system is based on the psychology of influence because it relies far more on persuasion and propaganda than on comprehensive education and conservative research. The "psychology of the sale" and persuasiveness of the system is most tragically evident when individuals become convinced they are sexual abuse survivors, even though they have no memories.

The term *persuasion* is often used interchangeably with the term *propaganda*, yet not all persuasion is propaganda.

28

The classical discourses and rhetorical methods of persuasion of the early Greeks and Romans were studied as forms for constructing arguments, debates or presenting cases for or against a proposition.

Propaganda originally meant the dissemination of biased ideas and opinions, and often lies and deception. It was not commonly used to describe thought control, brainwashing or persuasion tactics used by totalitarian regimes until World War I. Continuing study has resulted in a more subtle understanding of propaganda, and the understanding that it is not always used with purely evil intentions.

The term propaganda now includes mass suggestion or influence through the manipulation of symbols and the exploitation of individual psychology. Or, as described by Anthony Pratkanis and Elliot Aronson in their 1991 work, *Age of Propaganda*, "Propaganda is the communication of a point of view with the ultimate goal of having the recipient of the appeal come to 'voluntarily' accept this position as if it were his or her own."

How did you get involved in the issue of therapeutic abuse and coercion?

It was actually a natural progression from my work in the sociology, psychology and dynamics of violence and self-defense. The questions are fundamentally similar. In the psychology of self-defense the primary question remains: How are people groomed to be easy victims of violence? In the dynamics of therapeutic abuse the main question is similar: How are people coerced into accepting emotional and psychological victimization?

When I returned to college to finish my degrees, I was surprised by the near-saturation of 12-step psychology in counseling courses and among the students and instructors. It soon became clear that the boundaries between professional mental health services, pedestrian psycho-therapeutic systems, fundamentalist spiritualism and religion were seriously compromised.

After a particularly shocking college seminar, called "Counseling the Sexual Abuse Survivor," my concerns expanded beyond the collapse of boundaries between 12-step psychology and covert religious indoctrination in higher education. With the saturation of sidewalk psychology in mainstream society, it seemed extremely likely that the biased education and manipulative methods of information presentation being taught in seminars and colleges could create coercive counselors. Counselors educated in this manner could inadvertently harm clients, essentially repeating their own educational experience.

This course was almost surreal, and could have been billed as an extended psychodrama to show prospective counselors exactly what they should never do in counseling situations. With the exception of one other student, no one seemed to even worry that the counseling "techniques" taught might involve the use of aggressive suggestion, selective reinforcement, social reinforcement or social "proof" through group processes, manipulation via trance states, and other efforts to induce attitude change through tactics of influence.

The text for the course was the completely unsubstantiated survivors' manifesto, *The Courage to Heal*, by Ellen Bass and Laura Davis. The book is a collection of poems, stories, political rhetoric and opinions which may be helpful to some self-identified survivors, but is dangerous to people who are either unbalanced or searching for reasons to explain their problems or their unfocused anxiety. The authors write as if they have empirical proof that, "There are many women who show signs of having been abused without having any memories" (p. 71); "The body remembers what the mind chooses to forget"; "Memories are stored in our bodies" (p. 74); and, "If you don't remember your abuse, you're not alone. Many women never get memories. That doesn't mean they weren't abused" (p. 81).

The instructor told students to "suggest, affirm and validate" the near-total possibility that sexual abuse had occurred to any woman, regardless of her presenting problems. The instructor had written a 31-item list of "symptoms" of repressed memories. Ten symptoms indicated repressed sexual-abuse memories, and 15 symptoms indicated repressed incest memories. One of the items on the list: "A dislike for tapioca pudding, mashed potatoes and runny eggs."

Despite the obvious absurdity of the items on the symptom list and the outrageous content of the course, no action was taken to confront this kind of counseling education. When I took my concerns to the administration, I was told the issues would be "looked into," but further attempts to discuss the issues were politely ignored.

My protests seemed to have no impact and I thought the issue would end there. Then my research assistant saw a television program that gave the phone number of the False Memory Syndrome Foundation in Philadelphia.

At the time I did not realize that exactly the trend I had feared was already fairly well developed across the country. Clients were being influenced through hypnosis and various aggressive compliance techniques. They were coming to believe they were victims without memories; that buried within them were the memories of unimaginable atrocities; and that the grip of long-term amnesia could only be broken through therapy. I did not realize then that the growth of the FMS Foundation would herald the most explosive social-science controversy in decades.

What is the False Memory Syndrome Foundation and what is your association with it?

The False Memory Syndrome Foundation (FMSF) is a research-based organization dedicated to the gathering and dissemination of data, studies and literature on the full scope of the problems of child abuse, pedophilia, sexual abuse, social deviance and therapeutic abuse. Recent critics of FMSF have attempted to discredit its founders, with vague charges of alcoholism and claims that they are "perpetrators" because there have been allegations.

The FMS Foundation is concerned about the prevalence of bogus memory-storage and memory-retrieval theories and other scientifically illiterate, irrational and unsubstantiated notions promoted by ideologically over-invested therapists and writers.

In the short time that FMSF has been in operation, it has inspired productive controversy in the mental health community. I support the foundation because of the quality of the information they disseminate and the quality of the controversy they have inspired. But I am not affiliated with any organization, nor do I have an investment or a motive for promoting a particular position or agenda. My primary concern has always been unbiased education and responsible use of authority. The foundation upholds these standards. Of course they operate from the position of parents who feel victimized by aggressive therapies and various therapy cults. But they do not attempt to control information. Nor do they deny the prevalence of victims or the tragedy of sexual abuse and child abuse.

I heard that there is no such thing as false memory syndrome, and that the notion was invented by the False Memory Syndrome Foundation.

Contrary to popular criticisms of what is called the anti-therapy and recovery backlash, the concept of false memories was not invented to discredit sexual abuse survivors or to maintain societal denial about sexual abuse.

The term merely describes in common terms the possible results of therapeutic/client dynamics in which client suggestibility can be inadvertently or purposely exploited by the abuse of power, influence, trust and authority. False memories have both physiological and organic causations. They are also simply a product of the fallible workings of the mind, as well as a product of motives, perceptions and emotions.

The phenomenon has been studied for decades under numerous terms, such as *pseudomemories, iatrogenically induced memories, memory creation, hypnotic pseudomemory, hypnotic hallucinations, confabulation*, and most recently, *decades-delayed memory retrieval*. Most of the studies dealt with mental images and confabulations that emerged in controlled conditions, in subjects under hypnosis. Therefore, they require no explication here.

The term pseudomemory is commonly used to describe mental images that are believed to be memories that have been implanted in clinical studies or by informal suggestion in everyday life. The current works of Gail Goodman and Elizabeth Loftus are largely devoted to the studies of implanted and created memories in clinical studies. Loftus has found that even subtle suggestions can result in what are called pseudomemories. The definition of pseudomemory is plain and simple: a false memory.

Decades-delayed memory retrieval means that adults are recovering memories (usually in therapy) that had been totally unavailable to them for decades, or unearthing horrendous accountings of infanticide, multiple pregnancies, mass and serial murders, multiple rapes and ritualistic abuse perpetrated by organized, intergenerational cults of criminal satanists.

Iatrogenic illnesses or neuroses is listed in the *Dictionary of Psychology*, which was first published in 1968. An iatrogenically induced disorder is "a functional disorder brought on by the physician's diagnosis or suggestions." The term false memory syndrome is not intended as a legitimate diagnosis, but a description of a phenomenon. The term iatrogenic disorder is considered a legitimate diagnosis. If the symptoms of physiological diseases can be unintentionally induced by suggestion (disorders defined as psychosomatic), it seems that the symptoms of psychological disorders could be even more easily induced unintentionally by the therapist, the diagnosis or the treatment procedures.

Perhaps the identification of a "syndrome" with reference to false memories was premature, but the FMS Foundation is gathering data on both accused families and victims of therapeutic abuse who have renounced the mental images they constructed in therapy. Research is in process, hard data is being gathered and there is a growing pool of knowledge about influence, therapeutic dynamics, therapeutic ideology, and much more that is related to the problems. These efforts are increasing the possibility that if there is a distinct "syndrome" related to the phenomenon of false memories, it will be identified and scientifically recognized.

At first we heard a lot about post-traumatic stress disorder, then suddenly everyone was suffering from dissociative disorders, then multiple personality disorders. What are these conditions and how credible are they?

Post-traumatic stress disorder, as defined in the *Diagnostic and Statistical Manual III-R*, the bible for psychiatric diagnoses, is the development of characteristic symptoms following a psychologically distressing event that is outside the range of usual human experience. *Dissociation* is defined in the 1985 *Dictionary of Psychology* as the "separation from the personality as a whole of a complex pattern of psychological processes which may then function independently of the rest of the personality. The multiple personality illustrates dissociation in its extreme form. However, it is also present to some degree in hysteria, amnesia and schizophrenia."

The term "splitting" is often used by survivor psychologists to indicate dissociation. Bass and Davis define splitting to describe two different feeling states, the first is the "clinical" definition and the second is the "survivor" definition. In the clinical definition, splitting refers to the tendency to view people or events as either all-good or all-bad. It is a way of coping that allows a person to hold opposite, unintegrated views. In the survivor psychology definition, "splitting" describes the feeling the survivor has when she separates her consciousness from her body, or "leaves" her body.

Multiple personality disorder is the existence within the person of two or more distinct personalities or personality states. The inclusion of MPD in the *DSM-III-R* is still controversial because of disagreement in the psychiatric community regarding the legitimacy of the syndrome and the circumstances preceding its appearance. Until the early 1980s there were only a few MPDs documented in the psychiatric literature. Now there are tens of thousands, even though these have been diagnosed by a minority of counselors and therapists who consider themselves "specialists" in MPD and sexual abuse. Most therapists, psychologists, psychiatrists and mental health professionals never see a single case of MPD in their entire careers. The syndrome tends to manifest after long-term therapy, and most individuals diagnosed as MPDs are women, which raises more questions about the nature and focus of the therapy.

I used to hear a lot about the "inner child" on talk shows

and from celebrities in recovery. Recently I heard Roseanne Arnold talking about her "inner kids." What does this mean?

The concept of the "inner child" is fundamentally a metaphorical reference which suggests that unresolved childhood emotions hinder adult emotional development. The idea is that "if dependency needs are not met," people grow into adulthood with an "internalized wounded inner child" or a series of wounded inner children from different life stages. The notion existed long before it became commonplace. At first, recovering people were satisfied with the metaphor of one inner child. But with the rise of the multiple personality disorder diagnosis, these metaphorical "inner kids" are becoming entities, alters or distinct personalities. It should be no surprise, then, that many "recovering" people in time come to believe that they suffer from full-blown MPD.

Some therapists use the terms "emotional incest" and "covert incest." What do they mean?

The definition of sexual abuse used to be limited to overt acts of sexual touching and sexual acts, and obviously exhibitionistic and voyeuristic acts such as inappropriate nudity, masturbation, or other sexual acts (including the use of explicit language or erotic material with pedophilic intentions) on the part of the offender. Now it has been redefined to include "emotional incest," "covert incest," "boundary violations," and even has extended into the realm of psychic abuse, in which a child picks up "sexual abuse issues" from a parent who has been abused but is not an offender.

Sexual abuse theory has grown to truly Orwellian proportions. If the client reports "funny looks" or "icky feelings" when adults looked at her or him (as children), this is often reframed as sexual abuse. How is it determined that these facecrimes contained any sexual content or that the icky feelings indicated that incestuous thoughts had occurred in the looker? It seems to be based on the theory that "If you think you were abused, you were."

This process of reframing innocuous acts to determine abuse is highly directive. An act such as running bath water for a 12-year-old child, or bringing him or her a towel, can easily be reframed by a survivor psychologist as covert incest. And with the attitude of some survivor therapists—that covert abuse seldom or never exists without more blatant molestation—they may be more prone to assume that repressed memories lie behind the innocuous accountings of parenting behaviors given by clients. The danger of therapy-induced memories may rise proportionately to the degree to which such assumptions are held.

It seems like you talk negatively about the 12-step programs. I thought they helped a lot of people.

I have never said that the 12-step programs are always detrimental. What I am saying is that there are consequences and social repercussions for the widespread and uncritical acceptance of the 12 steps as a generic treatment for the human condition.

There is a gross coercion inherent in 12-step literature, 12-step dogma and 12-step-oriented curricula in higher education. The ideologies of 12-step recovery theorists have managed to become institutionalized without even much evidence in the way of controlled, longitudinal research indicating that the 12-step approach to addiction behavioral problems is truly the most effective method. There is no evidence that many of the problems addressed by 12-step programs are, in fact, addictions or diseases. Instead, the industry prefers to rely on testimonials and anecdotal reports, intuitive and spiritual ideologies, and the internally generated theories of a grassroots therapeutic movement led by self-professed alcoholics and addicts.

What are flashbacks?

The traditional interpretation of the phenomenon known as "flashbacks" was thought to be an uncontrollable process in which traumatic memory "blips," or scenes, begin appearing at random or in conjunction with memory triggers such as noises, odors and places. Flashbacks, as originally understood, began occurring shortly after a traumatic event. They were not known to be routinely, unconsciously and totally repressed for many decades and then suddenly begin intruding on normal consciousness.

World War I, World War II and Korean War veterans did not have the luxury of a legitimate diagnosis like "post-traumatic stress disorder" for traumatic overload. When these soldiers could not recover equilibrium after returning from active duty, they used to be called "shell-shocked." Society did not witness a mass movement of men from these wars entering therapy after warfare, only to discover that they had completely repressed the fact that they were traumatized by the conditions of war.

We have the same situation with the survivors of the Holocaust. These people were subjected to every imaginable horror, and we have not yet heard about survivors coming forward, only recently discovering they had been imprisoned in concentration camps.

According to anecdotes reported by survivor psychologists, however, flashbacks suddenly appear up to 30 years after an incident, and are often said to be evoked by external stimuli, to which the individual had been exposed many times without incident. This is not consistent with the flashback phenomenon as it has been established for decades.

Now that my daughter is "in recovery," we can't even

hold a conversation without her accusing me of being "in denial." What does this mean?

One of the primary defense mechanisms, coined by Freud, was "denial of reality," which meant protecting the self from unpleasant reality by refusal to face it. The concept of denial has surpassed this and similar previous definitions and now serves as an all-purpose diagnostic device in the recovery and survivor culture. The term also serves as a means to deflect critical scrutiny. Concerns for accuracy, research and professionalism are said to be motivated by "denial." Survivor psychologists deflect scrutiny, questions and criticisms by chastising the dissenters and claiming that they have "unresolved issues" of which they are "in denial." It has become politically incorrect even to question the wisdom of exaggerated, or simply fabricated, "statistics" of addiction, child abuse or incest.

My best friend told me she "found out" in therapy that she was an incest survivor. She told me she had no memories, but her "sensory memory triggers" helped her get in touch with what happened to her. What are sensory memory triggers?

In literature devoted to the neo-psychology of sexual abuse syndromes, the process of memory recovery has purportedly spread from being a common occurrence in therapy and in self-help or support groups to a spontaneous occurrence, thought to happen in conjunction with traumatic events, such as a divorce, a career change or other major passage. Sometimes these experiences are believed to be brought on by smells, colors and body positions that are supposed to be reminiscent of incidences of abuse. Sense memories, such as odors or impressionistic feelings of *déjà vu* in certain places or settings, are often called sensory memory triggers. Memories are also thought to occur during survivors meetings, while reading survivor manifestoes or watching television programs with sexual abuse themes. Other "memory triggers" include anniversaries of abuse, or observing children at an age at which the survivor/observer believes him or herself to have been abused.

I have heard you refer to the "neurotic language" of therapy and recovery. What do you mean and why is language so important?

Language not only reflects reality, it creates reality by changing the way we think. The neurotic language and compulsive labeling of therapy and recovery culture systems can make people get worse, not better.

In *We've Had One Hundred Years of Psychotherapy and the World's Getting Worse,* James Hillman asserts that therapeutic language and the talking cure of psychotherapy "makes language sick and therefore makes the world worse." Anthropologists, linguists and philosophers have long viewed language as a means to produce reality as well as a means to communicate about reality.

Learning the language and theoretical constructs of survivor psychology are the first steps contributing to the loss of critical thinking skills and precluding the acceptance of survivor logic. Survivor logic is supported by physiological fairy tales, urban legends, quack counseling techniques, bogus memory-storage theories and memory-retrieval techniques.

The sexual abuse/recovery movement has created its own jargon and internal logic to support the notions of "repressed memories." The movement has devised pseudo-psychological, theoretical constructs to support the processes of traumatic thinking and traumatic remembering. Though scientifically baseless, these have become standard learning requirements to participate in counseling, therapy, or self-help programs.

Such jargon tends to describe generally mundane physical conditions as "symptoms," and to reframe nearly the full range of family transactions in traumatic terms. Compulsively reframing your personal experiences in traumatic terms seems to lead to an unproductive neuroticism.

Could you explain how survivor therapists teach traumatic thinking, remembering and reframing?

Traumatic thinking, reframing and remembering are exaggerations of the more conservative therapeutic techniques of confrontation, cognitive restructuring and historical revisionism. Many survivor and recovery psychologists seem to believe that exaggerating these processes is necessary because of the power of denial.

Traumatic thinking, eloquently expressed by Hillman, is the process of learning the language, jargon, logic and rationale for reframing present reality or the past in dramatic, tragic, and emotionally charged terms.

Traumatic reframing or historical revisionism, is a process of indoctrination that usually occurs in a therapeutic or group situation. The individual's presumed "denial" is penetrated by persistent and aggressive attempts to reinterpret the individual's life story. Thus, a happy childhood becomes a "delusion," an apparently working family system becomes "dysfunctional," all parents become "abusers," and anything short of superhuman compassion and understanding becomes "abandonment." This is done by imposing a retrospectively-devised reality system which assumes that any pain or trauma was excessive and unnecessary and that if children grew up in less than optimum conditions, their growth and potential were severely stunted. The presumptions include the belief that they must be "reparented" or engage in "corrective experiences" through therapy or recovery work.

There's been a lot of talk lately about the power of suggestion with regard to therapy. Why now? Hasn't this always been understood as a powerful dynamic in the therapeutic situation?

The study of suggestion is not a recent concern in the field of psychology. It is, in fact, the fundamental issue on which the field is based. It is inconceivable to think that any mental health practitioner would not be aware of the power of suggestion, interpersonal cuing, demand characteristics (the power of the situation) and selective reinforcement.

In 1778, Anton Mesmer, a German physician, began manipulating trance states and treating numerous diseases with his theory of "animal magnetism." This theory hinged upon the notion, first put forth by the Greek philosopher Paraceleus, that the planets influenced the distribution of a "universal magnetic fluid" in the body which determined health or sickness. Mesmer seated clients around a tub containing chemicals and protruding iron rods. These rods were applied to diseased parts of the body. Mesmer darkened the room, played music that set the stage for trance states, then waved a wand and touched each client. Many claimed to be relieved of pain or other disorders.

Mesmer was discredited and drummed out of business, but in the 1840s his theories of suggestibility were revived by physician James Braid. Braid changed the terminology, describing suggestibility and trance states as "hypnosis," from a Greek word meaning sleep.

However, these historical accountings of the first documented use of manipulating trance states pertains only to the history of psychology. All primitive cultures used trance states, which were known to be naturally induced by repetitive sounds, storytelling, chanting, dancing, fire gazing and psychoactive plant consumption. It is well-known and accepted that shamans and healers, through the use of suggestion, both induced and "cured" hysterical conditions among their patients. The means by which they promoted and "proved" their theories were anecdotes and testimonies. When removed from the realm of primitive medicine and magic, these methods have long been considered the marks of quackery when used without credible supporting research and evidence.

My daughter told me that she found out in therapy that she can't remember parts of her childhood, that in her words, she's "missing blocks of time." According to her therapist, this means she has "repressed traumatic memories." Is it unusual to have incomplete memories of childhood?

The largely unsubstantiated and unresearched notion that "childhood amnesia" is a symptom of severe abuse is one of many supporting rationales for the recovered memory phenomenon. The idea that people have childhood amnesia because they do not remember "blocks of time" or have "missing memories" has been carried to absurd extremes.

Infant amnesia is a naturally occurring phenomenon. It is a lack of memory not due to forgetting, but due to incomplete stages of cognitive development, which provide no frame of reference for the storage of complete memories of events. Both infant and childhood amnesia are normal, well-documented psychological phenomena that do not necessarily have any relationship to trauma.

We do alter our memories to suit current belief systems. Painful memories are likely to be modified, exaggerated, minimized or dramatized. How a memory is synthesized depends largely upon what stage of resolution we have reached in our own lives. When we encounter the same dilemmas our parents faced, we often develop deeper insight and compassion. Thus the coloring, and sometimes even the content of memory, can be tempered through insight. Over time, most of us change how we feel; consequently, we change how we think—not only about today, but about yesterday. To the contrary, lack of resolution and insight may result in much less generous historical revisionism that also alters the coloring and content of memories, and reinforces the victim role.

Survivor therapists often say that everything that ever happened to us gets recorded in the cells of the body. Others stress that it is mostly traumatic memories that are recorded. Are memories literally recorded somewhere in the body?

If they are, it would certainly come as a surprise to molecular biologists, geneticists and physiological psychologists. Memory is a mysterious and fallible process. There are things we all remember whether we want to or not, and things we forget whether we want to or not. It is not always a conscious selection process, nor did everything that ever happened get "recorded," as espoused by survivor therapists. In *Repressed Memories: A Journey to Recovery from Sexual Abuse*, Renee Fredrickson discusses "five kinds of memory," claiming that all events are "filed" or "stored" by one of these modes. The following passage exemplifies the bogus survivor psychology notion of memory storage and retrieval:

> Her memories were inside her, recorded and stored in the filing system of her brain. They only needed to be accessed. Human beings have five kinds of memory. The mind has a process for recording, storing, and retrieving everything that happens by using at least one of these memory processes.

There may well be five kinds of memory, or many more, but memory does not function like a filing system, a videocamera or a tape recorder as claimed by survivor psychologists.

If anyone could truly discover how memories are stored, retrieved, lost or forgotten, it would constitute a revolution within the scientific community and in our understanding of mental and emotional processes, learning theory and human behavior. Until then, what we do know is that few memories remain unaltered by time and that memories cannot be literally accessed from "cellular storage," if, in fact, the cells of the body did "store" memories in the manner claimed in survivor folklore.

Have you met any people from the FMS Foundation that you thought were guilty of child abuse or incest?

Unlike many therapists who claim that they can spot "survivors" from across a room, I do not pretend to be able to perform psychic psychoanalysis. Usually within the first few minutes of talking with most of the accused parents, the common elements are apparent. First their daughter or son became involved in therapy, recovery or a survivors' group. There were often one or more precipitating stressors such as a divorce, career change or other major passage. Before long, the adult child is reading various recovery literature and often sending copies to the parents.

Then come the language changes. The adult child begins talking about "abandonment," "denial," "collusion," and "boundary violations." The adult child soon begins probing other family members about the past, often alluding to things that just "don't fit." Typically this begins with a sense of mystery, which then graduates to outright suspicion. (According to survivor psychologists, the "mystery stage" usually means the client is still slipping in and out of "denial.") Renee Fredrickson believes she is helping her readers through this transition by stressing the likelihood that those who are unsure are actually in denial: ". . . crippling disbelief is the hallmark of repressed memories. . . . Belief in the overt system is so strong that it is difficult to believe repressed abuse memories when they emerge. The family at first appears so accomplished, so stodgy, or so wholesome that it seems impossible for anything perverse to ever have occurred. The family myth of normalcy is extremely powerful."

In time, the clients cast off these "family myths" and identify with the survivor role. Many accused parents report that the adult child seemed to move into a new phase of mood swings and behaviors that were previously uncharacteristic.

Then one day "the letter" arrives, alleging past abuse in vague or highly specific terms. The stories may then evolve over time, invariably in the direction of more and more outrageous discoveries. Yet only rarely does an accuser confront his or her parents directly.

And still, it is only reasonable to admit that among the 10,000 members of the FMS Foundation it is possible that some percentage may be child abusers and pedophiles. Such offenders exist undetected within the general population as well. Bear in mind that the foundation concerns itself only with abuse allegations that hinge on the notion of wholesale repression and decades-delayed memory recovery.

My daughter gave me a "laundry list." She said it had examples of personality characteristics of survivors and "symptoms" of repressed traumatic memories. She said sexual abuse caused most of the problems the adults of today are having. Are these lists valid?

There is no research that proves direct cause and effect relationships between repressed traumatic memories to the numerous personality characteristics, neurotic tendencies or other problems on these lists. The 1993 statement issued by the American Psychiatric Association in response to the growing concern over memories of child abuse stated:

> Sexual abuse of children and adolescents leads to severe negative consequences. Child sexual abuse is a risk factor for many cases of psychiatric disorders, including anxiety disorders, affective disorders, dissociative disorders and personality disorders.

A *risk factor* and a *cause* are quite different. A risk factor alone does not cause a problem; it may contribute to a problem when other components and risk factors are present. This is not an attempt to trivialize the problems of victims. What needs to be addressed here is that the actual laundry lists being used to diagnose repressed memories are not based on any research. Most were simply fabricated or created by recovery culture converts turned overnight experts by virtue of personal observations and their own "recovering" status.

The laundry lists or checklists can be compared to the old "Barnum profile" used by psychologists since the 1950s. The original test was created by B.R. Forer in 1949 to test the fallacy of personal validation of personality test results. The test is used today to demonstrate the dangers of subjective and projective testing instruments to budding mental health practitioners. The types of statements made in the original Barnum profile are the same types used in recovery culture laundry lists or survivor checklists. The lists provide untested and unsubstantiated diagnostic criteria for various "diseases" and syndromes including sexual abuse, incest, repressed memories, and the presence of demons and alter personalities.

My daughter's therapist told me although my daughter had no specific memories of sexual abuse, she had nonetheless

"held the trauma at the cellular level." What does that mean?

The notion that "the body remembers what the mind forgets" lives on as one of the primary staples of survivor psychology. It follows from the already popularized (but erroneous) idea that the cells of the body "record" everything that happens in our lives. Survivor psychologists frequently state or imply that this recording process is somewhat selective and especially inclined to record memories of sexual trauma that are otherwise unavailable to memory.

Perhaps part of the difficulty in explaining "cellular memory" lies in the fact that science has recognized no such phenomenon in terms of literal memory storage. The term cellular memory is used as a metaphor in bio-psychology for the ability of cells to retain their genetic coding and to continue performing stable cellular functions over time.

To indicate the storage of traumatic memories, the term cellular memory is misused. Slanting the terminology to promote the bogus concept of "body memories" in the direction of scientific language is an attempt to sound credible. Cellular memory was never intended as a description of any type of "recording" of images or life events, either within brain cells, or within cells located elsewhere on the body.

The term body memory refers to the physiological manifestations of what is presumed to be a repressed memory, but may, in fact, be no more than a response to the stress of survivor therapy or of life itself. Such physiological responses include numerous ubiquitous problems such as rashes and headaches, and among women, vaginal pain, menstrual cramps or problems with the reproductive system.

The notion of body memory (as it is used in survivor therapy) is not to be confused with the idea that the body develops characteristic muscular and postural defenses or weaknesses in response to abuse, bad habits, injury or misuse. Body massage is sometimes is something mentioned without qualification as contributing to the recovered memory phenomenon. No legitimate physical therapist would practice psychology with a physical therapy license. That many massage therapists presume to have the capability to facilitate trauma-resolution with physical manipulation is extremely unfortunate for those who practice ethically, within the boundaries of the profession.

Attempts to link a poetic description—or analogy of cellular functioning—with any type of literal memory, are bogus and treacherously misleading!

Are some people more susceptible than others to developing false memories? Are there other factors besides bad therapy that may contribute to the development of false memories?

Of course. But the types of conditions that may result in false memories and false accusations are not generally well-known or understood outside of the mental health community. In fact, these conditions are often not well-known within the mental health community. The self-help culture is basically illiterate regarding medical and psychological causations for their behavioral and "spiritual diseases."

Hypnotizability and suggestibility can increase the possibility of false memory development. Hypnosis is a form of intense, focused alertness. The brain is experiencing a form of resting arousal, but the person is not asleep or even unconscious—even though high hypnotizables will enter this state so deeply that time is distorted and they cannot remember what occurred during hypnosis.

People vary in degrees of suggestibility. Depending on the situation, suggestibility can be manipulated in even resistant personalities. Two-thirds of the normal psychiatric outpatient population are hypnotizable; one-tenth are highly hypnotizable. Highly hypnotizable individuals undergo spontaneous trances, such as complete immersion or absorption in movies or books.

Many clients who have been diagnosed as having "body memories" may be suffering from *somatoform pain disorder,* or *somatization disorder.* This is defined by researchers Kaplan and Sadock as: "A chronic, but fluctuating, disorder which begins early in life, and is characterized by recurrent and multiple somatic complaints for which medical attention is sought but which are not apparently due to any physical illness." This is also the *DSM-III-R* definition, and the numerous complaints and interpersonal difficulties experienced by individuals with this disorder mirror the recovery culture laundry lists, and the sexual abuse and repressed memories symptom checklists. This disorder is often accompanied by anxiety, depressive symptoms and histrionic personality features.

Histrionic personality disorder may be preexisting in some clients who develop false memories or persecution syndromes. The histrionic patient uses emotional outbursts both to obtain attention and desired goals and to evade unwanted external responsibilities and feelings.

Conversion disorders also may be responsible for false memories, false accusations and imaginary victimization. Conversion disorders have traditionally indicated the transformation of a repressed impulse or psychological conflict into a physical symptom. In most cases the physical symptom or reaction cannot be traced to an organic problem, therefore the symptoms tend to be obviously hysterical conversions such as sudden deafness, paralysis or blindness.

In modern psychopathology, conversion disorders are no longer interpreted in Freudian terms. Freud believed that repressed sexual desires or other conflicts could be converted into physical symptoms. Robert Carson, James Butcher and James Coleman, contemporary researchers in psychopathology, explain that conversion disorders are now thought to perform a defensive function that enables a person to avoid a stressful situation without having to take responsibility for the avoidance.

Conversion disorders are thought to represent only 5 percent of all treated neurotic disorders. Psychologists say this is because a conversion disorder loses its defensive function when the absence of an organic basis can be shown. However, the new "symptoms" validated by survivor psychologists may have resulted in an epidemic of conversion disorders. Conversion disorders are likely to be reframed as "body memories" by survivor therapists, and attributed directly to a literal event that is presumed to have occurred in the past.

Survivor therapists have assiduously avoided the possibility that some chronically dissatisfied therapy patients are converting their own personal failures into physical and psychological symptoms as a means of avoiding responsibility. Then the assumptions of survivor therapy provide an explanation that transcends all others: repressed memories of trauma, even infantile abuse that you can't be expected to remember, becomes the *cause* for all problems. Repressed trauma theory even provides a reason for the existence of conversion symptoms and allows the client to abandon them because the responsibility has been shifted. This may account for some of the anecdotal reports of "healing" that survivors have reported. Even though some of them never got any memories, they did get a reason for all their conversion disorders and maladjustment issues.

Night terrors, or *sleep paralysis,* is a sleep disorder that affects about 5 percent of the population. People with the disorder wake up in the middle of the night paralyzed, and although they feel wide awake, they continue dreaming.

They often see demons, aliens or ghosts and are unable to distinguish these waking nightmares from reality. This disorder may be responsible for the "post-traumatic stress disorder" seen in individuals reporting UFO abductions and demonic rape.

One of the least known conditions that may result in false memories, false accusations and imaginary victimization is *factitious disorder*. This is defined as "the repeated, knowing simulation of disease for the sole purpose of obtaining medical attention." In its extreme form it is referred to as Munchausen syndrome, named after Karl Friedrich von Munchausen (1720-1797). Munchausen was a German cavalry officer who became famous for his colorful tales of extensive travels, which some historians say were largely fictional. Factitious disorder is accompanied by "Pseudologia fantastica," or an ability to tell intriguing and interesting tales of false accounts of illness, or tell other false trauma tales as ploys to obtain sympathy, such as falsely claiming deaths of relatives or loved ones.

Factitious disorder has traditionally indicated self-induced illnesses and feigned diseases or health crises. Although everyone has probably "played sick" at one time or another, factitial patients feign illness to pathological extremes. The term "malingering" was used commonly to identify a pattern of behavior used by military recruits to avoid active duty. The motive for malingering is fairly clear-cut. The motives of factitial patients are less clear. They appear to be motivated to obtain medical attention and unnecessary surgery, often at great physical risk to themselves. Research by Charles Feldman and Marc Ford, authors of *Patient or Pretender*, suggests an underlying brain dysfunction in factitial patients that may be related to the pathological lying and attention-seeking behaviors.

It would seem logical that factitial disorders would manifest in psychological as well as physical syndromes. Feldman and Ford report a tenfold increase in the incidence of published case reports of factitial disorders since the 1970s. Is it possible that social, philosophical and institutional reinforcement has created a cultural climate in which psychological as well as physiological disorders are aggressively feigned by disturbed clients as a means to obtain attention? The possibility should certainly be looked into, and the circumstances leading up to the diagnosis of MPD and repressed memory syndromes should be looked into as well. The majority of patients currently diagnosed as MPD, and a fair number of those diagnosed with repressed memory syndrome, have spent an average of seven to eight years in therapy and have gone through approximately five to eight therapists. They have been diagnosed with a variety of psychological syndromes. They have usually been treated with various psychotropic and psychiatric medications, yet have shown no long term or lasting improvement.

The MPD and repressed memory fad has therapists claiming formerly resistant patients are being "cured" or showing rapid improvement as a result of survivor therapy or personality reintegration therapy. Survivor therapists claim that this is evidence of former misdiagnosis and that the anecdotal claims of improvement prove the repressed memory hypothesis. Just the opposite may be true. Survivor therapists may be getting fooled by some of their clients—some of these people may show temporary but dramatic improvement as a result of intensive survivor therapy. Many histrionic survivors become small-time celebrities on the talk show circuit. Others are already celebrities. Yet if survivor therapy is going to prove to be a phenomenal success, the long term recovery of those diagnosed as suffering from MPD and repressed memory syndromes after years of therapy will have to be tracked and evaluated. If these people simply move on to the next fad in therapy, the assumptions of survivor therapy should be modified.

You refer to books such as *The Courage to Heal* and *Repressed Memories* as "factoid manifestoes." Could you explain this a little more?

The term *factoid*, credited to Norman Mailer, refers to a piece of information that becomes widely accepted simply because it has been asserted and repeated, sometimes through the media, often by an individual with some culturally valued signs of credibility such as an advanced degree. Information is persuasively presented as a "doctor's opinion" or a "professional opinion."

In other cases, manufactured credibility or the power of numbers is called upon to support the veracity of the factoid. For instance, Alcoholics Anonymous claims that "millions of people couldn't be wrong" about the efficacy of the 12 steps, instead of providing hard data that steps will work for *anyone* who works them.

Factoid manifestoes are books, lengthy statements, treatment plans or brochures that are made up of a series of factoids and presented along with deceptively authoritative-sounding words and phrases. Symptom lists, or laundry lists, of numerous behavioral "diseases" or repressed memories can also be classified as factoid manifestoes, insofar as they purport to offer medical or psychological advice and information based entirely on subjective observations.

Therapists routinely deny implanting false memories, calling the charge absurd, even impossible. I have heard quite a few therapists vehemently insist, "We don't even know how to implant false memories." When they say they have no motive to do such a thing, most of them seem sincere.

I do not like to use the terminology "implant" with reference to the co-creation of false memories between client and therapist. Therapists denying that they implant memories are really engaging in semantic squabble, but one with which I must agree. Therapists don't implant memories, they engage in an interactive process with the client that can result in the creation of mental images, which come to be identified as memories, or cause clients to develop a very strong belief in their unremembered victimization. This process involves numerous interactive transactions, and the client is influenced over time. Clients must come to first accept the premise that they have repressed memories that are the cause of numerous problems. Clients may come to therapy with this assumption, which still does not absolve the therapist of the responsibility to consider other options and proceed with extreme caution.

Other factors in the co-creation of memories include, but are not limited to: interpersonal cuing; indoctrination in the foundational beliefs of survivor therapy; numerous tactics of influence, including selective reinforcement of so-called traits or symptoms of repressed memories; implied or promised rewards tied up with excavating abuse memories; psychological intimidation and disapproval when the client disagrees with the diagnosis, inferences or beliefs of the therapist. In more extreme cases, there is actual physical abuse and restraint, including forced or coerced hospitalization and erroneous suggestions involving the literal interpretation of dreams, trancework, regression therapy and forms of hypnosis.

When the therapist believes in the probability of sexual abuse and uses erroneous information to diagnose repressed memories, it is presumed necessary to be persistent and aggressive in order to penetrate the client's powerful "denial" so that the mind and body will stop "holding" repressed memories "in storage."

Denial can be very powerful when there has been sexual

abuse, but the notion of denial can result in a no-win situation. Clients who have no memories are "in denial." Clients who claim they were not victims of sexual abuse are "in denial." Both those falsely accused and justifiably accused deny all allegations, so everyone is "in denial."

Ironically, therapists who claim they do not know how to implant or co-create false memories or mental images are actually admitting they don't know how *not* to co-create false memories in vulnerable clients. It probably cannot be stressed too strongly that the field of psychology was originally founded on the study of influence. Biological and organic theories of how behaviors and beliefs evolve took precedence over the fascination with influence until between 1908 and 1924, when social psychology, the scientific study of human behavior, emerged as a distinct branch of psychology. Social psychologists study why people do what they do; what processes people go through in order to make decisions; how behavior is shaped by others; and to what extent beliefs and behaviors are influenced by observing or manipulating the individual's decision-making processes, or controlling or observing the effects of group dynamics on behavior and attitude change.

It is unacceptable and completely absurd that anyone purporting to practice psychological counseling would be unaware of the vast body of research regarding influence, attitude change, manipulating belief systems, sales psychology, effects of authority on attitude change, and how belief systems are influenced by group dynamics.

Therapists who claim that it is impossible to influence clients to the point of false memory creation, or claim no responsibility for the co-creation of false memories or mental images, are undoubtedly very sincere. They are also revealing the depths of their scientific illiteracy, even their lack of basic common sense. Everyone knows that people can be convinced, or become convinced, of things that are not true, and that people construct "memories" of things that never happened. Therapists who have unwittingly engaged in aggressive memory recovery therapy based on the erroneous assumptions of survivor therapy may also be highly threatened right now. It is probably extremely difficult to come to terms with the realization that one may have been responsible for creating or exacerbating a problem instead of facilitating a resolution.

Some therapists may have to face the fact that the assumptions of survivor therapy may have prevented seriously disturbed clients from actually getting the kind of help they needed. There may be consequences to deal with, and much remedial work to be done to rectify those damages that can be determined to be direct consequences of survivor therapy. Any therapist who is capable of altering a potentially destructive course of therapy and embarking on a much more conservative course deserves to be acknowledged for having the courage to face this difficult transition and the responsibilities this action implies.

Chapter Four

Promises and Propaganda: How Survivor Folklore Plays upon Fears

Truth should not be defined by what people believe. . . . When we reach a point that what's true is what people believe, then we've sunk to a very dangerous way of thinking.

— Harold Goldstein
National Institute of Mental Health

Survivor psychology has contributed to the belief in a culture of perpetrators obsessed with victimizing their own young. Many survivor truisms are the products of "urban legends," or socially contagious hysterias. Urban legends have traditionally been rumors, sometimes based on grains of truth, that spread rapidly and persist despite obvious absurdity or even lack of proof. Sociologists have traced this kind of rumormongering to collective cultural anxiety. Although urban legends are always circulating, they tend to explode with a vengeance during times of great social change and upheaval.

Primal fears, unrealized hopes, dreams and deep psychological conflicts make up the content of most urban legends. Demonology and deliverance by symbolic acts of atonement are the oldest methods of diagnosing, and "treating," almost any problem or illness. The organized resurrection of 13th-to-16th century superstitions in mental health systems shows that technological sophistication is no defense against the monsters we create. If anything, the combination of high-powered marketing strategies and the media's near-total access to the public furthers the rapid spread of urban legends.

As more professionals develop attentional biases and become predisposed to seeking out and supporting repressed incest and satanic cult abuse memories, more cases are reported and then sensationalized through the popular media. This contagion trend is consistent with documented hysterias, shared delusions and the beliefs in demonology that have manifested in stressed populations from 300 B.C. to the present.

The contagious quality of archetypal representations of universal human fears in reaction to social upheaval and stress is evident in the "dance manias" that swept across Europe in the Middle Ages. Without benefit of media coverage, an "epidemic" of raving, dancing and convulsions affected groups of people in various parts of the country. The dance mania was believed to be caused by the bite of a spiritual tarantula, hence was referred to as "tarantism," and also "St. Vitus Dance."

Mass hysterias are reported infrequently in modern times, but they do occur. One example is the West Bank hysteria of 1983 in which hundreds of Palestinian school girls manifested symptoms of poisoning. The illnesses were initially thought to be the work of Israeli terrorists, yet later concluded to be of psychological origin.

Psychological fads are powerfully influenced by the cultural context in which they arise and the social reinforcement they are given. Every age has its pathologies, the scourges onto which a society projects its worst fears, its internal conflicts and stresses. The mental illness fads and disorders of modern society increasingly incorporate multitudes of ancient and contemporary hysterias. Rumor-panics, mental illness fads, unusual emotional disorders, UFO abduction stories and other obscure urban legends have a way of growing and persisting through media sensationalism.

Lately, the trend to reinforcing, encouraging and "treating" disorders formerly recognized as delusional by the majority of psychiatrists, scientists and academicians has spread. Harvard psychiatrist John Mack recently contacted 100,000 mental health professionals and urged them to take the "psychological aftereffects" of individuals reporting UFO abductions seriously. Writer Jem Sullivan says Mack believes that millions of Americans may have experienced UFO abductions and they become ". . . more troubled when an attempt is made to place their cases in a familiar psychiatric category, or to attribute their experiences to some other sort of trauma."

Rima Laibow, a New York psychiatrist, agrees. In 1989 she founded an organization called TREAT, which stands for Treatment and Research of Experienced Anomalous Trauma. Anomalous simply means deviation from the normal order, form or rule. Laibow began taking stories of UFO abductions seriously when one of her patients showed signs of "post-traumatic stress disorder" after seeing the cover of Whitley Strieber's alien abduction book, *Communion*. Laibow began looking into alien abductions, spiritual traumas, out-of-body experiences, possessions, attacks by demons, telepathy and other syndromes believed to be "paranormal traumas."

Laibow now believes people reporting encounters with aliens or ghosts deserve "quality psychological assistance," a view shared by Mack. Their rationale for believing these reports and taking clients absolutely seriously? *Patients will be further traumatized if they don't.* This is the same rationale used by therapists specializing in recovered or constructed incest and satanic ritual abuse memories. This rationale is dangerous, despite the fact that unconditional support may be essential to the therapeutic relationship. Therapists who become "true believers" in repressed memories (or the existence of highly organized satanic cults and UFO abductions) may unwittingly reinforce delusions caused by chemical imbalances, panic attacks, night terrors or other psychological and physiological disorders.

All claims of memory recovery or child abuse are not in dispute, nor is it in dispute that many people truly believe they have experienced alien abductions or demonic rape. What is at issue here is the wisdom of enthusiastically and seriously "affirming" such accounts instead of facilitating the client in stabilizing, either chemically or emotionally, and dealing with reality. Criteria do exist showing which memories are more likely to be false, the inadvertent results of the methods, manners and beliefs of therapists, and of untrained people acting as therapists. But survivor psychologists, almost by definition, tend to downplay the importance of even trying to distinguish fact from fantasy.

Expecting professional discernment is not the same as suggesting that clients be accused of lying or callously treated. The dominant concerns are that clients are not harmed by aggressive therapeutic modalities, families are not torn apart and that clients are not led, coerced or used to support the therapist's beliefs in rampant pathology. The client's psychological integrity and ability to face reality should be honored and cultivated.

Rumormongering in the Information Age: Factoids and Phony Statistics

The practice of reporting hunches and estimates as factual data or reliable statistics in regard to the prevalence of sexual abuse, rape and incest, became a common practice during the 1970s and 1980s, in response to probable underreporting of sex crimes and child abuse in the past. "Erring on the side of the victim" was the well-intentioned rationale for this practice.

The trend to inflate statistics is evident in the reports by the National Committee for the Prevention of Child Abuse. The committee states that between six percent and 62 percent of women are molested before the age of 18. An error factor of more than 59 percent should be cause for concern. So should the committee's observation that the most common estimate, stating that one out of four women will be a victim of sexual abuse, has become accepted as fact merely by repetition.

Recovery and survivor psychology are built on such use of factoids and manufactured statistics. In most cases, recovery and survivor authors quote each other authoritatively, taking the unfounded estimates, theories and assertions proposed by other 12-step theorists and survivor psychologists as facts. Many recovery, survivor and medieval psychology authors present lists of recommended reading, and some list a few references in their books. But such elements as footnotes, direct quotes, and overall emphasis on research are practically nonexistent.

Instead, recovery culture and survivor psychology theories begin as a collection of factoids which evolve into factoid manifestoes. A case in point, *Adult Children of Alcoholics Syndrome*, a 1985 book by Wayne Kritsberg, postulated the factoid that "over 50 percent of those raised in alcoholic families are to some degree in chronic shock." Kritsberg cites no studies and gives no references supporting the idea that a "syndrome" for being an adult child of an alcoholic even exists.

The 50 percent figure has a way of resurfacing. In *Secret Survivors*, E. Sue Blume states that "50 percent of survivors have no memories." If 50 percent of survivors have no memories, how was it ever determined that they were survivors? Still, the figure could easily slip by the reader without a second thought. After all, the "50 percent" figure is casually used to assess everything from rain probabilities to which team might win the Super Bowl. Yet even weathermen and football prognosticators offer more evidence for their claims than most recovery and survivor authors do for their unusual descriptions of mental and memory processes.

Another frequently quoted factoid is John Bradshaw's claim that 96 percent of all family systems are dysfunctional. Bradshaw later upped the ante to 100 percent during public seminars. Given the ambiguous subjectivity of "dysfunctionality," it is hard to know exactly what Bradshaw means to say about human nature that hasn't already been lamented by psalmists and philosophers for centuries. Neither does Bradshaw feel a need to address the logical absurdity created when everyone is abnormal, or dysfunctionality is the human condition.

Bradshaw expounds upon eating disorders with the same dogmatic certainty when he claims:

> Americans are killing themselves with food through overeating, starving, vomiting and improper diet. Eating disorders are addictions based on the denial of emotion, especially anger. A commentary on this condition is the fact that around 60 percent of women and 50 percent of men in this country have eating disorders.

This unsubstantiated "fact" would undoubtedly come as quite a surprise to researchers in the field. Although both anorexia and bulimia have risen in the past three decades, the reported incidence rate in the total population is two in 100,000. As with all statistics, the average of high-risk and low-risk populations is calculated. Bulimia may be present in 15 percent of college-age females, which is the group with the highest risk.

The connection between eating disorders and sexual abuse, incest and "repressed memories," has been "proposed in a growing body of literature," according to researchers Harrison Pope and James Hudson, eating disorder experts who reviewed the literature. To test this theory they embarked on a scientific review of the body literature, which suggests that these factors are causally related. The researchers assessed:

> Controlled retrospective studies comparing the

prevalence of childhood sexual abuse among bulimic and control groups. Uncontrolled retrospective studies of the prevalence of childhood sexual abuse in samples of 10 or more bulimic studies. Studies of the prevalence of childhood sexual abuse in the general population, which were chosen to match as closely as possible in methodology the available studies of bulimia nervosa in geographic location, age, and ethnicity of subjects, interview method, and criteria for defining childhood sexual abuse.

Pope and Hudson noted that although uncontrolled studies have reported high rates of childhood sexual abuse for bulimic patients, when general population studies are examined carefully and definitions of sexual abuse matched as closely as possible, the rates of sexual abuse among bulimic patients are closely related to the rates reported in the population at large. The researchers concluded: "Current evidence does not support the hypothesis that childhood sexual abuse is a risk factor for bulimia nervosa."

Although no empirical evidence links sexual abuse as a direct cause of eating disorders, numerous survivor psychologists claim that high or low body weight, dieting, binging or neurotic relationships with food are indicative of repressed abuse memories or sexual abuse issues. Even anxiety about body weight, or high levels of exercise, have been listed or discussed in survivor literature as "symptoms" of sexual abuse or repressed memories.

Identifying Characteristics of Factoid Manifestoes

Factoid manifestoes are complete works that are composed of false or fabricated theories or subjective philosophies parading as facts. The following criteria for the identification of factoid manifestoes is an amalgamation of Carl Hovland's model of persuasive messages, the propaganda theories of Elliot Aronson and Anthony Pratkanis, and my own observations regarding the way in which information is presented in recovery and survivor literature.

Factoid manifestoes can be identified by several factors:

1. *References, studies and sources are not used at all, or if references are listed, they are rarely cited.* Factoids and fabricated statistics given by undocumented sources are quoted liberally. Opinions are often reframed as facts.

2. *The writer takes advantage of basic human psychology, appealing to our deepest fears and most irrational hopes.* The language is florid and manipulative, but the concepts are repetitive and simplistic.

3. *The messages must be simple and repetitive so that they are more easily learned, and more likely to be accepted as true.* The message is packaged so that it attracts and holds attention.

4. *Incentives must be built into the messages to motivate action and attitude change.*

One of the most successful factoid manifestoes of all time is the "Big Book" of Alcoholics Anonymous. Nothing in the book is actually substantiated, but credibility is borrowed by the testimonies of several doctors who were quoted in such a way as to imply that AA is the ultimate solution for alcoholism. The Big Book was conceived in the spring of 1938 by Bill Wilson.

The 12 steps, the heart of AA's program, were an expansion of the "Six Tenets" of the Oxford Group, an AA precursor founded by right-wing evangelist Frank Buchman. As Charles Bufe documented in his book, *Alcoholics Anonymous: Cult or Cure?*, Bill Wilson and Robert Smith were Buchmanites in the early years of their sobriety.

Although AA would seem to owe much to Buchman's spiritual-reform approach from which the 12 steps descended, Wilson and Smith eventually distanced themselves from the Oxford Group and edited the contributions of its founder out of AA history. The separation followed a politically damaging interview Buchman gave to the *World Telegram* in 1936, in which he defined good government as a "God-controlled fascist dictatorship," and spoke admiringly of Adolf Hitler, whose rebuilt Germany was just beginning to hit its stride.

With this unpleasant "family secret" buried, Wilson and Smith were free to proselytize Buchman's theory—that alcoholism was a "spiritual disease," curable only through religious conversion—as their own. They did this with the help of some all-important qualifiers, such as officially downplaying the importance of organized religion and stressing that God only meant "God as we understood Him."

Such phraseology has proven adequate to convince most AA members to this day that the program is "not religious but spiritual." That this description has remained the party line surely would have gratified Bill Wilson, who went to his grave wondering if AA's religious overtones had alienated large numbers of alcoholics who might otherwise have sought help. And although AA is not representative of the same evangelical Christianity that characterized the Oxford Group, its insistence on a "Higher Power" has alienated many.

One must wonder whether these appeals to a generic Higher Power, and the Big Book's inclusion of a "Chapter to the Agnostic" (which many atheists and agnostics within the program find gratuitous and offensive), represent anything more than a desire on the part of AA's early members to appear open to all persuasions of religious belief and unbelief.

Yet the Big Book is replete with themes of confession, absolution and "spiritual awakenings" throughout. Perhaps many AA members and the public have confused the meanings of "non-religious" and "non-denominational." Dr. Foster Kennedy, one physician recruited to attest to

AA's effectiveness in an appendix to the Big Book's third edition (1976), observed: "This organization of Alcoholics Anonymous calls on two of the greatest reservoirs of power known to man, religion . . . and the 'herd instinct.' "

What the doctor neglects to mention is the fact that these two great "reservoirs of power" can easily be abused—and have been, by an endless parade of quacks and con artists throughout the centuries. The implication that God is behind—or highly approves of—a given product, course of action or ideology is among the oldest and most effective sales-psychology tools ever used. For some, that implication is all that is needed to sell the idea, action or product. Once some people have responded, their loyalty to the given product or ideology (AA in this case) becomes a kind of social "proof" for the inherent truthfulness of what is being sold or promoted and helps to draw others in.

The Learning Model of Persuasion

Part of what makes the journey of recovery so worthwhile to those who undertake it is its prepackaging into "stages," and the promise of psychological rewards for arriving at each new stage.

According to the 1949 research of Hovland, Lumsdaine and Sheffield on persuasive messages and mass communication, learning takes place in four stages of psychological processing. Hovland's learning model of influence is as follows:

1. *The message must attract the recipient's attention.* Ignored messages fail to persuade.

2. *The arguments in the message must be understood and comprehended.* In order for persuasion to occur, we need to grasp the point the speaker is making, whether it be the meaning of a simple advertising slogan or a complex set of reasons for why a nation should go to war.

3. *The recipient must learn the arguments contained in the*

message and come to accept them as true. The task of the advertiser and other persuaders is to teach arguments agreeable to the cause, so that the arguments will come easily to mind at the appropriate time and place.

4. *We act on this learned knowledge when there are beliefs and an incentive to do so.*

The difference between the basic learning model and the characteristics that identify factoid manifestoes is that the learning model could be adaptable for both positive persuasion and ideological propaganda, and the factoid manifesto model can only be used for ideological propaganda.

Elements of the learning model of persuasion are evident in the literature approved for distribution by the World Services Board of Alcoholics Anonymous. In the early days of the AA movement, the primary reward promised for maintaining long-term sobriety was the "serenity" achieved by religiously practicing the 12 steps and observing the 12 traditions. The promises have since multiplied as rapidly as 12-step treatable diseases have been propagated through 12-step theorists. In Bradshaw's 1987 book, *Bradshaw On: The Family*, working the 12 steps is related to "life beyond the ego," "transcending ego" and "transcending ordinary ego consciousness." Why is this objectionable? Because, like the concept of serenity, the notions of transcending ego and transcending ordinary ego consciousness do not really indicate a state of being that we can discuss without using more spiritualistic jargon, which may sound meaningful, but is indecipherable without *faith*. There is nothing wrong with faith, but AA purports to be a non-religious sobriety system and a recovery system for numerous behavior problems. The kind of blind faith required to accept the promises of "serenity" and "life beyond the ego" belongs in the realm of religion.

Implied in Bradshaw's claims about the egolessness achieved from living by the 12 steps is the notion that there is something fundamentally wrong with having an ego. And like all religious systems that claim that egolessness is some sort of divine or holy state of being, no one has ever demonstrated what this means, how egolessness is superior, and how this superiority is expressed. Since Freudian terminology has been integrated into our language, the word ego implies that psychology is being discussed, while the use of words like "transcending" and "consciousness" are wholesale religious ideas that rely on faith alone. It seems deceptive to use words in a manner that implies a science is being discussed when it is really religious psychology.

The implied rewards built into learning models of persuasion are even more prevalent as a tactic of influence in survivor psychology literature. Survivor psychologists are notorious for claiming that "memory recovery" will bring enormous rewards that cannot be achieved by any other method but forcing yourself to believe that your parents were pedophiles, sadists or pathological child abusers. Both extreme and trivial conflicts and problems are claimed to be caused by "repressed memories." Fredrickson's factoid manifesto, *Repressed Memories: A Journey to Recovery from Sexual Abuse*, shows the adept skills of its author at making definitive—but unsubstantiated—claims, and making promises contingent on your willingness to pretend, confabulate and accuse your parents of heinous crimes. If Fredrickson's statements were based on scientific research, her statements would not be so manipulative. Through the use of an autohypnotic technique, Fredrickson attempts to sell the reader on the idea that she may have repressed memories: "Let yourself know what the most hopeless or shameful problem in your life is. Try saying to yourself three times a day for one week, 'I believe this problem is about my repressed memories of abuse.' "

In the first place, why would anyone want to believe

they had been sexually abused or that their parents were sexual perverts if they had neither believed that or "known" it before therapeutic indoctrination? The motivation to believe is built into the traumatic programming of survivor therapy both by implied and stated promises. In this case, the implied promise is not exactly subtle: You will be able to get rid of the most shameful or hopeless problem in your life, if you can just dig up a horrible memory of sexual abuse or incest.

Once you start the process of "memory recovery," the coercion to continue at any cost begins. Fredrickson wants to make sure everyone has a fair chance to become fully identified with victimization: "Let your pain be your guide. Focus on your repressed memories for at least a year." But if you have no memories, how can you "focus" on them? You must be engaged in the process of creation and confabulation in order to manage such a feat. The sheer persistence of aspiring survivors and their therapists is amazing and terribly tragic. What if that kind of energy were focused on something socially or personally productive or truly healing to the heart and soul?

For those unsure that recovered memories are likely to be confabulations, consider the following definitive statements by Fredrickson:

> You never get repressed memories back by trying to remember them. If your memories are going to surface, you must look for them by piecing together clues from your past, your feelings, your dreams and images, and your body.
>
> Repressed memories also never feel the same as recall memories. You will not have the sense of having experienced the abuse you are remembering. Expect your repressed memories to have a hazy, dissociated quality to them, even after working with them over an

extended period of time. You will gradually come to know that they are real, but not in the same way you remember something that was never repressed.

Fredrickson explains away the fact that there are no memories, then proceeds to describe how a concerted effort can create constructed memories. She creates all kinds of expectations about how constructed memories are supposed to feel. This anticipates any future questions the client may have concerning the reliability of such memories, or feelings of unreality in connection with them.

The Propaganda Model of Persuasion

The propaganda model of persuasion, as gleaned from common elements in popular survivor literature, can be recognized by several elements listed below. Examples of each factor in the propaganda model will follow the list under italicized subheadings.

1. *The use of factoid statements.* Factoid statements often begin with tentative statements or questions, then conclusions are generalized from limited evidence. Complicated arguments follow, so that the person loses track of the original question or tentative statement. All this is followed by a statement of certainty, as if the point had been proven conclusively.

2. *Feigned skepticism, or a "conversion" story in which the social proof became overwhelming.* The author or therapist became a "believer" in the prevalence of dysfunctionality, repressed memories or satanic ritual abuse and the pressing need for techniques to help the masses "get in touch" with their traumas.

3. *Missing information.* What is not said is often far more essential than what is said.

4. *Imprecise language and loaded terminology* which allows manipulation of both facts and fallacies into sensible-sound-

ing doctrine. The false becomes true by association with facts.

5. *Manufactured statistics, the power of social proof and implied authority.* Such tactics help close the sale.

6. *Emotional and personal testimonials* that cannot be refuted without attacking another's subjective assertions or feelings.

Let's examine each element of the propaganda model as reflected in survivor literature:

1. *The use of factoid statements and complicated or convoluted arguments.*

An example of the effective use of AA propaganda is the factoid statement that AA has "saved millions of lives." This statement is one of the most frequent propagandistic statements made by AA promoters and converts, yet no evidence exists that this statement is true.

The use of testimonials, or "social proof," are present in survivor psychology manifestoes as well. Both types of promoters are absolutely emphatic that AA converts or survivor psychology clients "get better" or undergo miraculous changes by "practicing the principles" and engaging in the processes deemed necessary for "recovery." Since it cannot be proven that the AA program is unparalleled in its effective treatment of numerous behavioral and chemical disorders, and there is no evidence that the principles of survivor psychology bring about miraculous results, both systems rely on a version of the McDonald's slogan. Instead of "millions sold" they claim "millions saved," yet AA's claim is less reliable than the estimates of hamburgers sold by the McDonald's chain.

Both the AA movement and the survivor movement teach prospects and clients that public testimony is the key to recovery. Public testimony is also the key to self-persuasion. It has been well-known among social psychologists for decades that those who can be tricked, coerced or convinced into persuading others do a bang-up sales job on themselves in the process.

Another very effective factoid legend is that alcoholism, and, in fact, every behavior or process that has been designated a "disease" by 12-step theorists, is caused by "spiritual bankruptcy." This thesis is supported by indecipherable arguments, such as the one in the following passage by John Bradshaw:

> One thing was clear from the beginning of the A.A. movement. And that is that true recovery only ensues when one has had a spiritual awakening. Bill W. and Dr. Bob were clear about the ultimate problem of alcoholism. For them it was "spiritual bankruptcy". The disease of the disease is spiritual barrenness. This is what I have described as a hole in the soul—the problem of co-dependency. This ism of alcoholism or any addiction is the inner self-rupture called variously, internalized shame, self-will run riot or co-dependence. Each is a way to describe spiritual bankruptcy.

Using jargon to define and explain jargon is typical of coercive systems. Phrases such as "the disease of the disease," "self-will run riot" and the "ism of alcoholism" describe absolutely nothing.

George Orwell, author of the futuristic novel *1984*, warned us to be suspicious of words and phrases that do not bring pictures to mind. The basic premise of *1984* was that manipulation and destruction of the language could bring about total thought control and reality control. Yet Winston, the protagonist, refuses to lose hope. In his forbidden diary he writes, "Freedom is the freedom to say that two plus two equal four. If that is granted, all else follows."

This captures the conflict of the 12-step programs. Higher

Power equals God, and the 12 steps equal religious doctrine. Until the 12-step programs stop pretending to be non-religious tools for those with behavioral, chemical and emotional problems, and admit they are religious conversion organizations that happen to address these problems, everything that follows induction into the 12-step religion is simply more deception. As Richard Andersen noted in his book, *Writing that Works*, ". . . the degree of inhumanity in many destructive acts is usually proportionate to the language created to cover them up." The fact that survivor psychologists cannot explain their theories or methods without reverting to social proof, political ideology, deceptive language and jargon should be noted when evaluating the veracity of their claims.

2. *Feigned skepticism or a "conversion story" in which the social proof became overwhelming and the author or therapist became a "believer" and thus, a promoter.*

Robert S. Mayer is the author of *Satan's Children: Shocking Accounts of Satanism, Abuse and Multiple Personality* and *Through Divided Minds: Probing the Mysteries of MPD—A Doctor's Story.*

Satan's Children describes Mayer's pivotal encounter with an "MPD" named Rebecca who walked into his office one day and spontaneously began to "abreact atrocities." Mayer had previously seemed to attract an inordinate number of MPDs to his private practice. He had pioneered the MPD movement with a conference he sponsored himself; had appeared on *60 Minutes* with "Toby," his first MPD patient; and he had already published *Though Divided Minds* in 1988. Yet, during the writing of *Satan's Children*, he is claiming he still had "doubts" about MPD, presumably manifesting as a defense against satanic ritual abuse memories. Mayer recalls, ". . . it all seemed so farfetched," that is, until he met Rebecca. Mayer ruminates on Rebecca and his own "resistance" in the following passage:

> I argued and argued and argued with myself about
> Rebecca. I must have re-thought her case a thousand
> times. I was considering other psychiatric disorders.
> Was Rebecca malingering, desperately feigning an ill-
> ness for some other gain? . . . Society abounds with
> people who bankrupt themselves to acquire status sym-
> bols that supposedly confer peer approval. Psycho-
> logical needs often overrun logic.

Mayer reports that he is skeptical of Rebecca's claim to have given birth five times while still in high school. All five, she claimed, had been killed in cult rituals. Mayer did not believe this either.

Then the pains began, shooting up and down Mayer's right leg from hip to toes. Doctors could find nothing wrong. A massage therapist told him he was "hard as a board," and chased his aches and pains all over his body. Soon Mayer's massage therapist began developing aches and pains. Mayer finally concludes he is suffering from *secondary* post-traumatic stress disorder from his work with Rebecca and previous multiples because he had not fully believed them. He concludes that Rebecca gave him the disorder, which he then gave to his massage therapist. His massage therapist reportedly "discharged it" by spending hours on a cross-country ski machine. Mayer remarks, "God knows who got it next after Arne released it into the atmosphere."

Now Mayer is prepared to understand evil. He concludes that he has to stop denying the feelings his client's abreactions were bringing up in him. In order to help them change, he must become a believer.

Renee Fredrickson's conversion story follows the same formula as Mayer's. While doing "marathon therapy workshops" in Dallas several years ago, she claims the partici-

pants were regularly recovering "buried" memories of molestation and incest. She wonders if this phenomenon isn't
some kind of "contagious hysteria" and ponders the possibility that sexual abuse and incest in the South might be a
consequence of the Southern patriarchal system. She reports finding out that "repressed memories" are as common in the Midwest as in the South. Fredrickson states:

> Like sexual abuse in general, the more you know about
> what to look for with repressed memories, the more
> you find. Just as client's stories of incest were met with
> skepticism and controversy, I found many people were
> skeptical about client's repressed memories of abuse.

Fredrickson is angered to find that the psychological
literature has nothing on repressed memories. She claims
that case histories of sexual abuse told to Freudian analysts
were still being reinterpreted in Freudian constructs such
as "penis envy" and "castration anxiety." Like Mayer,
Fredrickson must go it alone and sponsor her own lectures
on memory repression. Expecting about 10 people at her
first lecture, she was astounded when 120 people showed
up. She taped the lecture and offered it for sale. It sold all
over the country by word of mouth. By now Fredrickson is
convinced of the enormity of the problem, and reports:

> Millions of people have blocked out frightening epi-
> sodes of abuse, years of their life, or their entire child-
> hood. They want desperately to find out what
> happened to them, and they need the tools to do so.

Mayer's and Fredrickson's conversion stories incorporate a number of elements from the propaganda model of
persuasion. They both use factoid statements, draw conclusions generalized from limited evidence, and present con-

voluted or indecipherable arguments after which statements of certainty are made. They both claim to have been skeptics, who were converted to believers on the basis of social proof. The social proof convinced them that there was pressing need for their services and the so called techniques, or "tools," they offer to help their clients remember trauma.

Rima Laibow's conversion story follows a similar progression. Laibow says that for years she thought that notions of alien abduction were "psychotic." In 1988 a patient she had known for many years came into her office in a panic after having seen the cover of a popular alien abduction book out of the corner of her eye. The patient supposedly did not know the content of the book, but soon began having terrifying memories of encounters with creatures like those on the book's cover. Laibow was certain her patient showed no other signs of psychopathology and decided she showed the symptoms of post-traumatic stress disorder. While Laibow continued to treat her patient, she puzzled over the existence of post-traumatic stress disorder in the absence of external trauma. After researching the field of UFOlogy, Laibow concluded that "there are things in the atmosphere that we call UFOs that appear to have physical reality."

Laibow feels that only trained clinicians should be treating patients with UFO abduction trauma, possession stories, demonic rape trauma and so on. She may be right. However, clinicians who truly believe that these "anomalous events" are literally visitations from space aliens and demons, when there is absolutely no evidence apart from anecdotal accounts, may be encouraging neurotic and psychotic delusions. Professionals who become believers may fail to treat chemical imbalances that cause bodily sensations and delusions, or overlook whatever rational explanations may exist for such experiences. Finally, the notion that scores of people need to have their delusions, fantasies and bodily sensations "taken seriously" is ridiculous if the goal of psychological counseling is to help clients make healthy and functional adjustments to reality.

3. *Missing Information. What is not said is often far more essential than what is said.*

According to Fredrickson, "millions" of people have blocked out portions or all of their childhoods. We are led to believe that this is a logical conclusion based on her continuing discoveries of "repressed memories" in clients. However, her "techniques" for discovering repressed memories involve selective attention and selective reinforcement of so-called "symptoms." Fredrickson explains:

> I began to listen to my clients with focused attention to the possibility of buried memories. Strange dreams, half-finished sentences, strong reactions to abuse issues, and imagery that persistently bothered my clients began to take on new meaning.

The moral crusade to prove that millions are afflicted with repressed memories of incest and childhood abuse is furthered by Fredrickson's simplistic logic and persistent sales tactics. She urges readers to overcome the "denial" that returns to haunt them. Fredrickson tells readers: "In reading this book, whenever you find yourself worrying—What if I'm wrong?—try to always ask yourself the opposite question—What if I'm right?" There are immense leaps of logic and missing information in Fredrickson's book. However, the most glaring omission is any type of documentation for her claims. None of her "discoveries" about the prevalence of repressed memories are substantiated, none of her memory storage or retrieval theories are substantiated, and none of her promises regarding the rewards of memory work are based on samples, studies or research.

Dr. Mayer's books have absolutely no basis in research either. It is particularly unfortunate to know that Mayer is so highly suggestible himself that he is "catching" his clients disorders and then passing them on into the atmosphere or to other unsuspecting victims via his psychic transmission theories.

4. *Imprecise or manipulative language.*

Clients of survivor psychologists routinely come to fit the profiles of "survivors" after they have learned what their "symptoms" are supposed to be. Then they produce "memories" in reaction to their presumed symptoms. This theme was repeated throughout a series of the structured interviews I conducted with mental health practitioners specializing in sexual abuse.

The question, "Could you describe the concept of body memories?" brought out a number of revealing patterns in which clients came to "discover" memories of abuse after therapists had interpreted their physical complaints as "body memories." But what *is* a body memory? Here is how one therapist answered the question:

> ... when someone's getting close to remembering something, they may have the beginning of the memory in their body. Or, for instance, I've had people in their wrists, with aching in their wrists have, you know, because that's come about later that they were held by their wrists, or during the abuse.

Many of the therapists' responses were less specific. Most were at least somewhat redundant—different ways of saying, "A body memory is a memory stored in the body"— without any precise attempt to explain the phenomenon in normal medical or psychological terms.

Here is how another therapist re-interpreted physical aches and pains as "symptoms" of hidden abuse:

> A body memory is a memory without cognitive awareness of its origin or ideology. It's consistent with some type of trauma where a person may have been forced in a variety of ways and physically held, pushed or subjected to some external physical coercion, such as a memory of someone's—a feeling like someone's hands are around her throat, or a sensation like something cylindrical is in her vagina, or severe lower abdominal pain, or lower back pain which later becomes a memory of the person's father lying with his erect penis against her lower back and those types of things.

The idea that common physical sensations or complaints later become specific memories of sexual abuse strongly suggests the influence of a survivor psychology-oriented therapist using traumatic reframing techniques. Human beings are afflicted with numerous somatic complaints. Among women, some of the most common are lower back pain, abdominal pain and various gynecological complications. The potential sources of traumatic memory construction through reframing such complaints into "symptoms" of sexual abuse are endless.

5. *Manufactured statistics, the power of social proof and implied authority.*

Once again, the Big Book of Alcoholics Anonymous provides an example. A statement by psychiatrist Dr. Kirby Collier, which appears in an appendix called "The Medical View on AA," demonstrates manufactured statistics, the power of social proof and implied authority:

I have felt that AA is a group unto themselves and their best results can be had under their own guidance, as a result of their philosophy. Any therapeutic or philosophic procedure which can prove a recovery rate of 50 percent to 60 percent must merit our consideration.

Implied authority lies in the wording of the statement: "Any therapeutic or philosophic procedure which can prove a recovery rate of 50 percent to 60 percent must merit our consideration." The fact that a doctor is talking about *proof* of results sounds very official, yet the "statistics" are simply pulled out of the air.

In *Uncovering the Mystery of MPD: Its Shocking Origins, Its Surprising Cure,* James Friesen uses another common propaganda tactic—the use of supporting information from "studies" that are not identified:

Two studies about the early lives of multiples came up with the same percentages—97 percent have been subjected to serious child abuse as youngsters. Another found that 88 percent had been abused sexually, with 83 percent having been sexually penetrated as young children!

If any such studies exist, they should certainly be correctly cited. Readers deserve to know the sources of "statistics" or information. If the purpose of a book is to inform and not indoctrinate, then sources will always be cited.

6. *Emotional and personal testimonials that cannot be refuted or argued without attacking another's subjective assertions or feelings.*

This propaganda technique is covered at length throughout this book because the survivor movement was spawned in the wake of the 12-step recovery culture, which relies on propaganda to perpetuate itself. "Breaking the silence" and publicly exposing traumas gained widespread acceptance as the 12-step network grew.

The survivor movement amplified this notion of healing with talk-show exposés and celebrity child abuse and addiction books. Now we have performing MPDs who change "alters" at will before television and satanic ritual abuse seminar audiences. The fact that these testimonials are public makes them harder to retract later. If people can be tricked or inspired to attest publicly to a belief, even if their own faith is lacking or shaky, they will be forced to try to reconcile their public statements with their inner experience. It is easier to try to appear consistent with your public statements than it is to retract public statements. Moreover, the public confessional styles encouraged in today's social climate offer ample opportunities to persuade yourself by persuading others. The rules of therapeutic talking have been integrated into the culture at every level. Sermons, diatribes, 12-step and survivor psychology testimonials are all delivered under the guise of "I messages." All a person has to do to derail a lively debate is start talking about his or her *feelings*. Television talk shows are often organized around family quarrels. Usually members of the audience get involved to deliver their own personal opinions of who is more right or wrong, or to participate in the name calling. By the time the show has reached, or nearly reached, its potential for chaos, someone unfailingly stands up and asks, "Have you had or considered counseling?" It is assumed that counseling is always helpful and that everyone could benefit. It is as if people have lost the ability to think or to handle the most basic, everyday communications on their own.

The Hypnotic Model of Persuasion

The hypnotic model of persuasion always incorporates the basic three-point formula of all social control modalities. A social control modality is any system or philosophy designed to control people by manipulating their emotions and their belief systems. There are three common elements to all forms of social control systems or modalities: Doctrine (rules and regulations); overload stimulus (prayers, practices, rituals, hypnotic readings, alignment with social institutions, invocation of the power of numbers, inflated claims of success, exploitation of fear); and last but most important—invocation of a higher authority. God is the primary higher authority used, but secondary authorities can be invoked as long as they are outside of the individual's discretionary powers. Similar dynamics are often brought forth in the therapeutic situation and are listed below.

1. *Learning the rules and regulations of therapy.* Clients must learn the language and logic of therapy and often sign contracts with the therapist regarding their behaviors and agreements. In responsible therapeutic relationships these types of agreements may be productive for the client. Therapeutic language and logic may be helpful in reasonable increments, as long as it is not presented as the only proper way to think and talk. However, many "survivors" must first be taught how to be survivors, to talk and think in the language of victimology and to identify with victimization.

The back cover blurb on *The Courage to Heal* exemplifies this learning and identification process. Beside the caption "Taking Stock," it is explained that the book "addresses the question 'Am I a survivor?' and outlines the effects of child abuse and how women cope over time." A woman goes to a therapist with a series of problems or conflicts that are causing her pain. She is distracted from her therapeutic goals by "learning" that her pain is really a cover-up for something much worse. Her confusion and pain are about something so horrible she doesn't remember it. It is always reassuring to find that the circumstances that cause you pain and grief are not your fault and that you do not have to actually do anything to change your circumstances. All you have to do is come to therapy and let the therapist take you back through the trauma that is presumably buried, and you will miraculously recover your lost childhood, your creativity, your true self and true potential, and probably lose weight in the process.

2. *Sensory, emotional overload.* The client is often awe-struck by the therapist's supposedly superior adjustment and technical or mystical knowledge. Therapists often create an atmosphere with incense, music, hypnotic tapes, ocean sounds or other soothing sounds, lighting, crystals, "sacred" objects, framed slogans on the walls and so on. Creating a relaxing or healing atmosphere is desirable, unless the therapist has an improper agenda and the client is highly suggestible. A hypnotic atmosphere can contribute to sensory overload when clients are bombarded with sensory stimuli, "message units" or information that they are unable to evaluate critically.

It is often assumed that a hypnotist must be very skilled in order to perform complicated inductions, that an individual must consent to hypnosis and that some people cannot be hypnotized. None of these assumptions is true. On the other hand, the notion that people cannot be hypnotized against their will is generally accepted as true by hypnosis experts, but suggestibility can be heightened by therapeutic dynamics. Survivor and recovery therapists use a number of techniques that result in inadvertent hypnosis. This means that clients can become highly suggestible through relaxation techniques, age regressions, trance writing and various types of psychodrama.

The means by which formal hypnosis is induced is so simple and so commonplace that it happens naturally. Trained hypnotists learn a "patter," the content of which often has nothing to with inducing hypnosis. The point of the patter is to override critical thinking skills by sensory overload and boredom. The content of the pre-induction patter often contains rapid-fire nonsense, or what is known as translogic or trancelogic. When the hypnotist maintains a paternal or maternal attitude and authoritatively talks in circles, not inviting dialogue (usually the subject is instructed not to talk but to signal), the critical mind cannot process all the "message units" and sensory input. The hypnotist gives rapid-fire directions and actually tells the subject to do several things at once, but the subject is instructed to remain passive as well. For instance, the subject is instructed to relax and is then given both suggestions and mixed messages. The subject will be told to move an arm, but may also be told that no matter how hard they try, they will not be able to move the arm. Or they may be given suggestions in such a way as to imply that anything they do means they are under hypnosis. This scrambles the usual defense mechanisms, and the mind shuts down and becomes hypersuggestible in order to cope.

Hypnosis is a form of boredom, or escape from the pressures of the situation. It is also a conditioned response, and in our society we have been conditioned to believe that hypnosis occurs when the words "You are very relaxed" and "You are getting sleepy" are uttered. This is why simple relaxation techniques and guided imageries can induce heightened suggestibility whether the practitioner intends it or not.

When a counselor or therapist unintentionally brings about heightened suggestibility, the same progression of events may occur as in formal hypnosis. Many trance states are so subtle the client does not even realize he or she is in a highly suggestible state. Hypnosis is best described as a state of heightened suggestibility. It is not a somnambulistic state of robotic obedience.

Confusion about hypnotic techniques and suggestibility is not uncommon. The term hypnosis is actually outdated. According to Robert Baker, author of *They Call It Hypnosis*, the term hypnosis, as it is used today, is no more accurate than the terms mesmerism or animal magnetism, used 200 years ago. Baker says there is no such thing as hypnosis, at least "not as a unique state of awareness or consciousness." Factors that bring about attitude change include the power of suggestion, beliefs and expectations, social compliance, personal motivations or the desire to cooperate with the hypnotist or therapist. Baker disputes the fallacy that people are able to do things under hypnosis they could not ordinarily do—such as accurately remember everything that ever happened to them.

> They *do not* and *are not* able to do these things under hypnosis *any more than they can* do them when they are wide awake. In other words, motivated people who are wide awake are *just* as strong; our memories are improved a little when we, wide awake, close our eyes, relax and concentrate. But we do mix fact with fiction anytime we remember anything; and being *distracted* from the cause of the pain and *reducing the anxiety* surrounding the pain does reduce its intensity when we are wide awake. . . . In fact, most of hypnosis is nothing but *reassurance* and *distraction*.

Some therapists are particularly gullible regarding the special powers conferred on hypnotic subjects, or clients engaged in memory reconstruction in survivor therapy. It is assumed that everything brought forth in formal or informal trance states must be a true and accurate accounting of the facts, and that anyone claiming any type of victimization must be literally believed and encouraged to remember more trauma.

3. *Invocation of a higher authority.* One of the self-aggrandizing theories of contemporary mental health professionals is that they are the new "spiritual leaders" of our times.

The dynamics of social control modalities create a powerful cycle of reinforcement and social proof in which clients are rewarded and encouraged for validating the therapists' world views, and therapists are encouraged and rewarded as the process unfolds and their assumptions are reinforced.

Propaganda, Persuasion and Hypnosis: Information Overload

The propaganda model of persuasion and the hypnotic model are similar because they both rely on information overload, and exploit the human desire to avoid mental burnout, if possible. The therapeutic environment and the self-help meeting environment are highly persuasive, especially for people in crisis, who are sometimes incapable of processing more information or even dealing with simple tasks. The repetitive simplicity of 12-step meetings is often comforting—the same passages read over and over in respectful monotone, the same chanted prayers to open and close the meetings. People often do not even realize they are being influenced, and many believe that they don't even listen. Though repetition and an emphasis on uncritical acceptance (as implied by slogans such as, "Make yourself teachable," "Fake it till you make it," "Your best thinkin' got you here," "Utilize, don't analyze"), are in keeping with hypnotic persuasion, that does not mean their effects are always, or even usually, sinister. The point is, it is important to know something about the power of suggestion inherent in such innocent use of ritual and slogans. It is important to look at what messages are being conveyed, and finally it is important to know how these internalized messages affect thinking. Many of these anti-intellectual messages are also implied and stated in therapy. The purpose is to shut down critical thinking by shaming the client. These kinds of slogans—whatever their "utility" in helping to stop undesirable behavior—also strip people of autonomy and confidence, the very traits therapy and "recovery" should be cultivating.

To summarize the elements that bring about heightened suggestibility, the following list exemplifies the hypnotic model of influence:

Distraction and reassurance. A client who fears hypnosis is distracted and reassured by the therapist who re-labels the attempt to produce heightened suggestibility as a "relaxation technique" or a "light trance."

Sensory, emotional or information overload. The client comes into therapy speaking common language and the therapist begins talking psychobabble or begins a hypnotic patter. The language is "loaded," or full of jargon. The result is confusion—hence, receptivity. Therapeutic talking is as much about obscuring meaning as it is about being "clear."

Double-bind messages.

> Client: "I want to be a better person."
> Therapist: "You have to get worse before you get
>   better."
> Client: "I want to forget the past and move on."
> Therapist: "The only way out is through."
> Client: "I've suffered enough."
> Therapist: "You haven't experienced your legitimate
>   suffering."

Repetitious use of slogans and grossly oversimplified explanations of complex processes. Labels self-defeating (or therapeutically undesirable) thought habits as "stinkin' thinkin'." Denigrates thinking as inferior to "feeling" or intuition. "Your best thinkin' got you here," and "That's what you get for thinking." Makes pretenses to perfect understanding of highly complex processes such as memory and information storage. Consequently, notions such as "Your subconscious mind works just like a tape recorder" and "Everything that ever happened to you is recorded in your brain or body"—though false—have become therapeutic truisms.

Factoid Manifestoes, Projective Testing Instruments and the "Barnum Effect"

As previously explained, factoids are created when an inference, bias or theory is restated as a fact, or when vague or partially true information is combined with propaganda. Factoid manifestoes are collections of opinions, personal philosophies, ideology and persuasive appeals that are written in a manipulative and deceptive manner. The point is to give the impression that the "millions" saved are empirical proof of the inherent power in the philosophy, the principles or the fundamental correctness of the ideas.

Factoids and factoid manifestoes are often spontaneously invented or created, like the numerous laundry lists describing the "symptoms" of various disorders and conditions such as the traits of ACOAs or "workaholics."

The personality traits on the laundry lists of the recovery and survivor movements, and the diagrams plotting the progressions of the various diseases and recovery processes, are crude and imprecise projective testing instruments.

Projective testing, as it is used here, means two things. In one scenario, clients are asked to create artwork, do collages, paint or write stories, which are then interpreted by client and therapist. This creates dialogue. Insight is thought to emerge from this process. In scenario two, clients take various "personality tests," or go through crude inventories of presumed "symptomatologies."

Other types of projective tests are called Thematic Apperception tests in clinical psychology, and simply personality tests in other counseling systems. These types of tests involve a task that is interpreted by the therapist. The client may finish sentences, or look at pictures and write a caption or title for the picture. The client is sometimes led to believe that the results of the task are interpreted scientifically and actually reveal deep secrets about him or her. However, there is nothing scientific about the results of these tests, even the ones that have been used for decades. The interpretation is purely subjective, but like gypsies and fortune tellers looking at lines on the palm, believers must assume there is something there that reveals their innermost secrets. The trust and expectancy created opens the doors for questions, by which the therapist gauges the client's current mental and emotional state.

Projective testing instruments are supposedly used in the mental health field for the purposes of conservative diagnoses, or to encourage communication. However, these types of tests, or identification tools, in the hands of ideologically overinvested survivor psychologists allow vague and changeable diagnoses, by which almost anyone could be described at any given time. Many critics would prefer that projective testing instruments be removed from professional practice because of the overwhelming evidence that the results can be so easily manipulated or interpreted to suit any agenda. Specifically, projective tests have the greatest potential for imposing biases and coercing confabulated testimonies of abuse.

Yet, projective tests are the instruments of choice in the newer counseling fields dealing with sexual abuse, codependency, satanic ritual abuse and dysfunctional family systems. The lists of "traits" are inferential, claiming that completely unrelated aspects of personality and behavior are caused by past events. Now people who cannot remember being abused are being taught that their excessive weight, lack of education, lapses of memory and social isolation are symptoms—perhaps even proof—that abuse must have occurred.

The original laundry list for Adult Children of Alcoholics was written one day in 1978 by an "adult child" named Tony Allen for an Al-Anon group he attended in New York. The laundry list describes assumed personality characteristics that supposedly resulted from living with one or more alcoholic parents, or even with parents who were not alcoholic, but were, themselves, raised by alcoholics. Tony's list quickly grew in popularity, and became the touchstone for many of the factoid manifestoes about "adult children" that are published routinely with little or no research.

Basic insecurity and socialized tendencies to intellectual timidity make people easy marks for quack-promoters of behavioral diseases. Yet recent research has indicated that these all-inclusive descriptions of characteristics are no more accurate than predictions made by fortune-tellers or astrologers.

In one such study, Sher and Logue isolated the traits claimed as indicative of an "adult child of an alcoholic" from recovery culture literature and combined these with "Barnum statements." Barnum statements and personality tests are designed to draw out the tendencies of most people to identify with vague personality "traits" and statements regarding self-esteem. Statements such as "You have been disappointed in love" or "You have advanced rapidly in some areas of your life, but in others you are underdeveloped" are examples of Barnum statements. Most people agree with these statements because they tend to be generically true. This is known as the Barnum Effect.

Sher and Logue combined the ACOA personality traits with previously tested Barnum statements. These were administered as a new personality test to 112 adult children of alcoholics and 112 adult children of non-alcoholic parents. About two-thirds of the participants from both groups identified with both sets of statements, whether they were ACOA or Barnum statements.

These results point out the universality of human conflicts and insecurities, and how easily these can be exploited. It also points to the dangers of assuming that subjective analyses are correct when, in fact, these lists merely illustrate the similarities in human experiences and emotional conflicts.

Parallel Motivation, the Placebo Effect and the Previous Investment Syndrome

As we look at the potential dangers of coercive therapies, it is also useful to examine alternative explanations for the enthusiasm of the participants themselves. The concept of parallel motivation is a variation of the placebo effect. A person in counseling or self-help programs is motivated to change or to "feel better." This motivation is the primary reason change occurs, and when a program and a person are in sync, the outcome is improvement. However, people who are truly motivated to change will do so without any support whatsoever. Support is often just a way to affirm a decision. The foundation is personal motivation.

Because of a socialized tendency to fear our own power and deny our own efforts, it is often more emotionally and psychologically acceptable to project power and success onto outside forces. Often people simply feel better by taking any sort of action in which the expectation of improvement has been created. This is the placebo effect.

Another psychological factor that chains people to ideas

and courses of action is the previous investment syndrome. This is a variation of cognitive dissonance. Once a person invests time, money and energy in a course of action, and then publicly attests to its positive effects, it is difficult to change courses. This appears to be because people do not like to be wrong or inconsistent.

Therapeutic Values, Ideals and the Inevitability of Failure

The therapeutic party line among survivor and recovery psychologists is that certain behaviors are unhealthy because they are "chronic, progressive and fatal." Life is chronic, progressive and fatal. The notion that people die of "codependence," "relationship addiction," "sexual addiction," and various mundane behaviors such as shopping and fantasizing, shows the extremes to which the ideology of therapy has compromised the public's thinking skills. Many recovery culture and therapeutic publications are full of superficially logical material that, on closer examination, makes absolutely no sense.

The same problem appears in survivor literature that typically tells us absolutely nothing factual about sexual abuse or survivors. Instead, they exploit and glorify the pain and horrendous recovery journeys of "composite" survivors, all the while setting up hooks to convince the average woman with conflicts or problems that she too is a survivor of something so horrible that *she doesn't remember anything*. However, if she would try to remember, and construct a victim story, then *nothing in her life up to this point was ever her fault*. This nearly pathological need to shift blame, or even assume that blame must be placed, is not liberating to women at all. True survivors must come to terms with the fact that childhood sexual abuse was not their fault. Yet survivor therapy carries this idea much further and ties every feeling, action, mistake, failure and

96

even success to some underlying inadequacy stemming from both repressed and remembered abuse.

This tendency to internalize emotions, argues psychologist and therapy critic James Hillman, is among the most seductive—and vicious—hooks in the never-ending labyrinth of therapeutic thinking. Feelings about any present condition or social issue must be converted into metaphors for "unresolved issues" from the past.

In *We've Had a Hundred Years of Psychotherapy and the World's Getting Worse*, Hillman and coauthor Michael Ventura analyze the therapeutic assumption that feelings, traumas and events must be "processed" or "dealt with," as if the therapeutic process really could "transform" these experiences. Hillman says that our hardships are the raw material of our creativity, our drives, ambitions and passions. Therapy, he contends, is a "consumer's ideology" that assumes you can either "get rid" of conflict or "transform" it into something useful. Hillman is one of the few critics of therapy who also fully recognizes the need for what he calls "soul-making." Soul-making has nothing to do with popular therapeutic ideals or values. It is not a process of learning conformity, but a process of becoming more individuated. Hillman says the soul finds itself through its pathologies. He encourages a fearless inner journey, which is not the same as the "fearless inventory" and public confession rituals of therapy and 12-step systems.

Excessive focus on feelings and thoughts without a solid sense of purpose stemming from productive action is destined for failure. Self-help writers who claim that "changing your thoughts will change your life" have done more than think. At the very least they have marketed or charmed or bulldozed their way onto the lecture circuit, so that they could be in a better position to tell the public that their lives could be changed by thinking correctly.

To some extent, how you feel or choose to feel does determine how you think, act and function. But these theories have been used like a one-way ticket to submission. Rhetorical concessions are made to the individual's power to make an impact on the world. But, usually, these actions are limited to acts of thought.

The philosophy of "thoughts as things" has a long history. The recovery version is illustrated in the following passage from John Bradshaw:

> Our beliefs create the kind of world we live in. . . . I can create a different world by changing my beliefs about the world. Our inner state creates the outer and not vice-versa. It took me 42 years to learn this simple spiritual principle. Codependence is at bottom a spiritual disease because it believes exactly the opposite. The core belief of codependence is that my inner state is dependent upon what is outside of me.

This is a perfect set-up for dependence in pursuit of unattainable therapy and recovery ideals and rewards, which are held out like a carrot on a stick. There are no problems which cannot be solved by "changing your beliefs." Therefore, if you continue to be vexed by problems, it must be that you're still stuck in codependence. Moreover, if our beliefs create the world and not vice-versa, then believing in multiple manifestations of "spiritual diseases" is creating those diseases! If Bradshaw really believes his statement, he could better serve humanity by thinking alcoholism, human suffering and child abuse out of existence instead of inventing and exaggerating human deviance and social pathologies.

Why Would Any Therapist Want to Make People Lie?
What is often mentioned in reaction to the so-called

"backlash" against the recovery and therapy movements is that, considering the scope of the sexual abuse problem, it is inconceivable that therapists would try to make people lie.

What is rarely mentioned is that *making people lie* has nothing to do with the dynamics of coercive therapies. Coercive therapists do not want to make people lie. Instead they believe that the truth is buried, and that getting to this buried truth is the way to best help the client. Although much coercion is inadvertent, any mental health practitioner who denies or is unaware of the processes of attitude change, memory and historical revisionism, influence, motivation, interpersonal cuing, suggestibility, demand characteristics, situational cues, selective reinforcement, client therapist or situational expectations, behavioral modification, compliance tendencies, confabulation, fantasy proneness, histrionic personality disorders, high hypnotizability, and organic and personality disorders that cause confabulation needs to go back to Psychology 201. That degree of construct illiteracy in a mental health practitioner would be comparable to a practicing surgeon who doesn't know basic physiology.

Few critics believe therapists try to coerce clients to lie. But the history of influence and recent research into therapeutic dynamics has revealed that some therapists coerce clients to perform in accordance with their expectations, and that the process by which this happens is rarely intentional. The use of inherently hypnotic techniques, with preexisting expectations on the part of the therapist (and the client), along with reinforcement and interpersonal cuing, can bring about iatrogenically-induced symptoms and syndromes.

Changing beliefs and behaviors through the tactics of influence and the power of authority is based on simple cognitive and emotional principles. It is not at all difficult to locate research on the effects of somatic, auditory, visual, emotional, interpersonal and situational cuing, and manipulation of suggestibility through hypnosis. However, we are badly in need of literature for the general public that encourages critical thinking skills and explains how the psychology of influence works—as opposed to *using* the psychology of influence *upon* the public in order to sell a product or promote an ideology.

A word of warning: The ways in which human needs, emotions, motivations and fundamental psychological principles can be manipulated and exploited are probably endless. Your best defense is knowledge of the tactics of influence, the psychology of sales and the characteristics of quackery.

Chapter Five

The Survivor Machine: Ideology, Sales Psychology, Slogans and Cognitive Restructuring

Science is teaching man to know and reverence truth, and to believe that only as far as he knows and loves it can he live worthily on earth, and vindicate the dignity of his spirit.

—Moses Harvey

T he theories of survivor psychology, and those of the recovery culture in general—of which survivor psychology can be regarded as a particularly strident, literalistic and often evangelical extension—started out harmlessly enough. It seems logical that children would learn about themselves, the world and relationships from parents and primary caregivers. It is emotionally appealing to believe that if you "go back" and metaphorically rescue yourself from situations that were beyond your control as a child that you could develop greater compassion, understanding and self-esteem. It is supposed to follow that having compassion for yourself gives you a greater capacity for compassion for others. These theoretically simple steps do have merit and emotional healing potential, but it seems that a huge abyss exists between theory and application. This is especially true in sexual abuse psychology.

As you will see in the many quotes and examples to follow, some survivor therapists and authors tend to be patronizing and manipulative. The pages of survivor manifestoes practically drip with contrived sympathy, trumped-up claims and soft-sell tactics. If this sounds unsympathetic, it is not intended as such. It is sometimes necessary to be brutally honest when the stakes are high. In this case, stopping the emotional and psychological abuse inflicted under the guise of therapy is the goal.

"The Only Way Out Is Through"
Two main organizing principles of recovery culture and

survivor psychology are: (1) Internalized shame from original abandonment causes inauthenticity, which must be denied because the pain of being conscious of fragmentation, inner splitting and falseness is too great to bear. Thus, the state of denial is the limbo in which the masses live, unaware of the losses of their "true selves." (2) In order to heal the inner splitting, or spiritual bankruptcy, one must come, or be coaxed, out of hiding through the progressive self-exposure system built into the 12 steps and some recovery-oriented counseling systems. The relevant slogan is, "The only way out is through."

There is no question that introspection and grieving can be healing processes, but an aggressive and unnatural focus on "walking" through past trauma and "abreacting" it may inflict the primary trauma. The theme of resurrecting and literally reliving trauma, and walking through traumatic memories, repeats itself again and again in survivor literature, always with implied rewards built in as incentives. It is also assumed that in order to begin stage two recovery, more aggressive techniques are required to delve into original pain work or grief work.

As John Bradshaw explains, "As we allow our shame to be exposed to others, we are exposed to ourselves. . . . We have to move from our misery and embrace our pain. We have to feel as bad as we really feel."

Recovery culture psychology and survivor psychology are similar in their memory theories, although in the early days of the recovery culture the childhood amnesia theories were not nearly as malignant and rampant as they are now. However, the notions of repression and denial in recovery culture psychology in the early 1980s served to lay the foundation for the total repression and childhood amnesia notions to take root in a dangerous and destructive manner. Now, the lack of memories of abuse is believed to be indicative of really horrible abuse.

The neo-psychology of sexual abuse syndromes builds a theoretical foundation on a number of questionable and tenuous assumptions. These assumptions include the following ideas:

1. You do not have to have any memories of sexual abuse to be a sexual abuse "survivor."

2. Many "survivors" never get memories.

3. If you *think* you were abused, or have a sense of being abused, you were.

4. The more severe the abuse or trauma, the deeper the "repression."

5. Victims must be unconditionally believed.

6. Any attempt to verify memories or question the credibility of accounts given is "revictimization."

7. Everyone suffers from childhood trauma, even if they are not aware of it.

8. This unconscious suffering is the underlying cause of all adjustment problems, which, in turn, ensures that the world is run by dysfunctional "adult children."

9. In order to stop unconscious repetition/compulsion of past abuse (self-inflicted, inflicted in abusive relationships) or "acting out" abuse (as an offender), one must enter intensive therapy in which all traumas are resurrected and compulsively repeated until the maximum emotional agony is expressed, and, in many cases, until the social and personal fabric of the lives of alleged victims (and their families) are completely destroyed.

10. Exposure of the alleged "perpetrator" is part of the "healing" process, often with little or no regard for consequences.

Reliving the pain

Literally manifesting and communicating with the metaphorical "inner child," or series of wounded inner children within, is the focus of 12-step recovery therapy. Non-dominant handwriting and numerous forms of psycho-drama are frequently used for the purpose of manifesting and then "reparenting" the inner child through various developmental stages. The reparenting efforts include buying toys and clothes appropriate to the developmental stages of the inner child as it "grows," buying a baby doll that represents the inner child and rocking it, cooing to it, repeating "affirmations" to the doll, feeding it, changing it, taking it on outings, and periodically asking the doll what it wants and responding according to the messages received.

The neo-Freudian idea that emotional and psychological development becomes "frozen" at developmental stages in which the "true self" of the child is "shamed" and forced into hiding was resurrected and popularized by John Bradshaw. The therapeutic technique of acting out past trauma through "grief work" and "original pain work" is based on the theory that trauma must be relived, felt and grieved in order to heal the "inner splitting," and integrate the denied and dissociated aspects of the self.

Robert S. Mayer, a self-styled expert in satanic ritual abuse and the prevalence of multiple personality disorder hypothetically caused by such abuse, tells an "MPD" client with "repressed" memories:

> Sometimes the only way around these things is through them. But I have to warn you, Randall, it won't be pleasant and it won't be easy. If there was any other way to help you without making you delve into all this, I would do it. But I think you know by now there isn't.

Mayer then ruminates on his client's past abreactions and concludes that these had only been partial. Mayer is certain that a successful abreaction must be complete with all of the feelings that should have been felt the first time. He rationalizes philosophically: "If these feelings are left behind again, they will continue to fester, like a partially drained boil that becomes reinfected." Like other recovery and survivor theorists, Mayer believes that in order to prevent reinfection, the survivor must undergo original pain work.

Original Pain Work

Original pain work is described by Bradshaw in the following passage from *Healing the Shame that Binds You*:

> We use the family system as a way for people to see how they lost their authentic selves and got stuck in a false self. As the person experiences how he got soul-murdered, he begins grieving.

This grief work, or original pain work, is undertaken to relieve the symptoms of post-traumatic stress disorder and chronic shock, which are the presumed results of having been raised in a dysfunctional family. Traumatic childhood experiences are compared to the experiences of soldiers who have been traumatized by the conditions of battle, according to recovery authors Wayne Kritsberg, John Bradshaw and Jane Middleton-Moz, to mention only a few.

The process of therapeutic thinking (or decomposition as "healing") is supported by the recovery/survivor psychology ideology of "getting worse before you get better." In current theory, the worse one gets, the better one is becoming. The better one becomes, the more likely one is to identify with lifelong pathological status.

Through indoctrination in therapeutic language and thinking, events that clients had previously considered non-abusive or even mundane become not only abusive, but intentional. "Walking the client through a memory" usually means formal or informal induction of a hypnotic trance state in which the therapist follows an aggressive script with the agenda of activating old pain or feelings of abandonment, neglect or persecution. Once these feelings are aroused, the intellectual indoctrination begins. The idealized version of how parents *should* have been there, and *should* have known all, and been all-protective and sensitive is "explored" until the client comes to believe parental failures were intentional to the point of malicious neglect and abuse. Part of the process of therapeutic indoctrination exploits the perfect and precious status and the helplessness of the child in order to get the client "into their feelings" about childhood persecution.

Thus, the therapeutic culture creates its own consensus reality system through anecdotes, language and the redefinition of emotional and behavioral norms. Exploring alternatives and a range of behavioral options and emotions is most certainly not inherently unhealthy. It becomes unhealthy when the world view of a therapist is pathologically-based, and the "exploration process" is a smokescreen for an indoctrination process.

The Impact and Power of Slogans

An important aspect of the 12-step approach and the survivor psychology method of treatment involves the power of talk therapy, confession and "inspirational" slogans. However, many of the slogans are designed to induce guilt and bypass critical thought processes. For instance, the slogan, "You're only as sick as your secrets," performs three functions: (1) It indicts personal integrity or privacy needs and boundaries. (2) It diagnoses pathology in anyone with secrets—in other words, all people. (3) It induces guilt and coerces confessions so that people can prove they are not "sick."

Recovery culture slogans often rhyme, which makes them

easy to remember, but rhyming actually performs a dual function. The use of rhyme and slogans are common in all systems of indoctrination, simplistic systems of influence or so-called "mind control" systems. Rhyming slogans do not even have to make sense to appeal to the emotions. Slogans tend to be a form of translogic, a word coined by John Kappas, founder of the Hypnosis Motivation Institute. Kappas combined the words trance and logic to describe the way that words are used in hypnotic inductions and hypnotic presentations. Translogic is a tool to bypass critical thought processes and access the subconscious or play on emotions and beliefs.

The use of slogans is common and does not, in itself, constitute a threat to normal suggestibility or consciousness. Slogans rhyme because they are easy to remember, not because rhyme is inherently a devious strategy used for the purposes of mind control. However, the excessive use of slogans, along with all the other methods of coercion and influence used in aggressive recovery and survivor therapies, appears to contribute to the loss of critical thinking skills among both clients and therapists involved in such therapies.

The many hypnotic, translogical and rhyming slogans used in recovery psychology often surface in survivor psychology systems, and many survivors are recommended to 12-step groups, where slogans substitute for both conversation and thinking. In addition to "You're only as sick as your secrets," the three most important recovery psychology slogans are: "Denying is lying," "You no longer have your emotions, your emotions have you," and "You can only heal what you can feel."

The progression that leads to receptivity to aggressive therapies is easily illustrated by the sequential use of the slogans. First, the individual becomes convinced that "secrets are sick" and that they do not have a right to personal discretion in revealing or concealing information. Then, "denying is lying" is used as a crowbar to pry more deeply into the psyche for repressed memories, to create anxiety when the person cannot produce such memories, or when the person fails to describe the past in traumatic terms. People who prefer to keep secrets or private thoughts to themselves, or those who do not remember any major trauma are thought to be classic examples of individuals "in denial."

Bradshaw manages to work two of the slogans into his pitch for "stage 2 grief work" in the following passage:

> Denying our emotions is a way that causes us to lose control over them. Once repressed and denied *you no longer have your emotions, they have you.* Denying is lying. You no longer have the memories, but the repressed emotions form a frozen energy core that *unconsciously runs your life.*

A little further into the pitch for stage 2 grief work, Bradshaw becomes emphatic, stating, "The only way out of this death style is to embrace the legitimate suffering. *You can only heal what you can feel.*"

This internally consistent series of confrontations leads directly to the assumption that a simple cause-and-effect system is in motion. The cause originated in infancy and early childhood, and the effects are repetition/compulsion patterns in adulthood. The only cure is reliving the original pain of the cause.

These are the same theories that drive the modalities of survivor psychologists and medieval psychologists. The same slogans that underscore childhood trauma and adult maladjustment also mandate "the cure"—working through this old pain which presumably prevents one from being healthy in the present.

Learning to think and remember traumatically is an essential part of the 12-step recovery process. In survivor and medieval psychology systems, the intensity has been turned up several notches. Once traumatic language is taught, the process of reframing the past or rewriting history to conform to a simple script begins. The script is a *cause-and-effect* plot line that inevitably leads to the same conclusion: Most of your psychic, somatic and emotional pain is directly related to past traumatic events that fester below the conscious level.

Historical Revisionism:
Traumatic Thinking, Remembering and Reframing—
The Cognitive Groundwork for Survivor Psychology

Pseudo-psychological jargon and slogans are used to reinforce therapeutic thinking, but jargon and slogans can also be a means of transmitting biases, and reframing the client's past and present experiences. For instance, the term abandonment no longer means desertion, it now describes any failure by the parent to respond to the child's "age-appropriate needs." The word "addiction" describes any behavior performed excessively or with "life-damaging consequences," but does not necessarily involve ingestion of narcotics or alcohol. The word "incest" can denote atmospheric "vibrations" that carry thought waves with a "sexual frequency."

Like the problems (as defined by survivor psychologists), the solutions have also become increasingly vague and mystical-sounding. One must "get worse before getting better," and "feel as bad as one really feels" as part of the process, or journey, to mental health. The notions include the belief that in order to get out of the misery, one must go through the misery.

It is well known in the field of psychology and counseling that the language of therapy must be learned in order for the client to engage in "cognitive reconstruction." Such paradigm shifting is a legitimate function of counseling and psychotherapy, but traditionally with less emphasis on proceeding "as if" incest trauma, soul-murder by parents, MPD, satanic ritual abuse or demonic possession were the foundation for nearly all adjustment problems.

Learning to think traumatically and reframe the past to suit a socially constructed reality system is a common ideological conversion technique. Exaggeration, disregard for facts and aggressive mental programming are not characteristic of professional mental health systems, particularly when combined with emotional hyperbole, lurid tales of abuse (used by the therapist as reassurance that recovered memories are true) and disregard for research.

When traumatic thinking and traumatic remembering are learned, the process of reframing family history in pathological terms begins. This commences with retrospective projective techniques, such as interpreting childhood artwork and family photographs. It progresses to non-dominant handwriting, "art therapy," trance writing and various hypnotic techniques. Diagramming the family system is another form of "inner-child" therapy. However, ancestors are not identified for their genetic contributions and the order of their appearance, but for their perversions, addictions and pathological status. Unfortunately, trying to diagnose long-dead ancestors as addicts, child molesters and codependents is generally little more than a process of confabulation, given the usual lack of hard evidence or information about previous generations.

The overzealous therapeutic modalities designed to uncover repressed memories are justified as being in service of the "protection of the children," and to stop the cycle of abuse. But as Lynn Gondolf, one of the first "retractors" of repressed memory therapy, observed:

There are a lot of crusaders out there and sure, the most honorable thing you can do is fight child abuse. ... But they (the therapists) want to do it with middle-class women. They don't want to work with low-income people who don't have medical insurance. Poor people can't afford repressed memories.

Soft Sell Tactics: Exploiting Neurosis— Constructing "Evidence"

The principles of exploitive sales psychology are based on a formula that is apparent in satanic ritual abuse books, "case studies," and various survivor manifestoes. The formula is a combination of the criteria that identify factoid manifestoes and the elements of the propaganda model of persuasion. These have already appeared earlier, but will be repeated in the section to follow for easy reference.

The formula for factoid manifestoes tells how factoid manifestoes manipulate information in order to influence. The propaganda model of persuasion goes into greater detail, pointing out more specific techniques used to influence. The single most important thing to consider when evaluating a message or an author's work and intentions is this: *Is the material designed to influence by persuasive tactics, or by solid information?* All authors and individuals are biased in some manner and hope to influence readers. Imparting information should be a primary goal, and influencing others secondary for an ethical professional. An exploitive sales psychologist will aim to influence at the expense of the truth.

The points that identify factoid manifestoes and the elements of the learning model of propaganda are shown below.

Characteristics of factoid manifestoes

1. *References, studies and sources are not used at all, or if*

references are listed, they are rarely cited. Factoids and fabricated statistics given by other undocumented sources are quoted liberally. When undocumented sources are quoted second-hand, they are often reframed as "facts," not opinions or theories.

2. *The writer takes advantage of basic human psychology, appealing to our deepest fears and most irrational hopes.* The language is florid and manipulative, but the concepts simplistic.

3. *The messages must be simple and repetitive* so they are easily learned and more likely to be accepted as true.

4. *Incentives must be built into the messages to motivate action and attitude change.*

The Propaganda Model of Persuasion

1. *The use of factoid statements.* Factoid statements often begin with tentative statements or questions, then conclusions are generalized from limited evidence. Complicated arguments follow, so that the person loses track of the original question or tentative statement. All this is followed by a statement of certainty, as if the point has been proven by convoluted arguments.

2. *Feigned skepticism or a "conversion" story in which the social proof became overwhelming.* The author or therapist became a "believer" in the prevalence of dysfunctionality, repressed memories or satanic ritual abuse, and the pressing need for techniques to help the masses "get in touch" with their traumas.

3. *Missing information.* What is not said is often far more essential than what is said.

4. *Manipulation of facts and fallacies* into propaganda whereby the false becomes true by association with facts.

5. *Manufactured statistics,* the power of social proof and implied authority.

6. *Emotional and personal testimonials* that cannot be re-

114

futed or argued without attacking another's subjective assertions or feelings.

If mental health professionals cannot understand or see through the manipulation inherent in these tactics, we are faced with a pandemic problem: lack of reasoning skills and severely stunted intellectual capacities. It is hard enough to accept that a fearful and needy public is being taken in by exploitive charlatans cranking out what one astute observer of the phenomenon calls "crypto-pedophilic pornography." Therapists themselves feign skepticism in tortured accounts of their early struggles to "believe," as their own lives begin decomposing from the emotional crisis caused by the therapeutic drama. The suggestibility of these therapists is frightening, their sales tactics are doggedly persistent, and their casual and continuous admissions of ethically reprehensible behaviors are shocking.

The logic and the patter of survivor manifestoes explains away why "survivors" often have no memories, why they will doubt what they have constructed in the process of therapy, and why it is all true just because they say so. The logic and patter are also a relentless con job to sell therapy, Satanism and severe dissociative disorders to the public.

It is almost as if some factions of the therapeutic population are so bored and jaded, their professionalism has been reduced to lurid satanic and sexual abuse fiction—sort of a therapeutic "virtual reality" that becomes indistinguishable from real life. The advancements in their therapy are enhancements in the technology of creating moods and eliciting psychodramas, supported as authentic by all of the available logical props and narratives.

In some cases, the therapeutic journey is a process of simple neurotic transference. The therapist seizes on a benign neurosis and encourages, reinforces, affirms, validates, suggests, sells and even insists, that the client *must* have repressed memories and must dig them up in order to be free, healthy, happy, successful, creative and productive.

In other cases, therapists are presented with a dilemma. Clients come into therapy full of preconceived notions and pathological labels from their involvement with the recovery culture. The therapist must struggle with the conflict between letting the client "have their own reality," even if it's unhealthy, and helping the client find reality through therapeutic confrontation.

The term "neurotic" is not necessarily a diagnosis of mental or emotional aberration. Most people are neurotic in one form or another. In its most common form, neurosis is merely a benign mental disorder characterized by (a) incomplete insight into the nature of the difficulty; (b) conflicts; (c) anxiety reactions. In its more serious forms, neurosis may result in personality impairment and in physical manifestations such as headaches, skin disorders, sleep disturbances or persistent delusions.

Since most people are at least slightly neurotic, exploiting neurosis instead of helping clients gain a better insight into their behavior is ethically reprehensible. It is routinely denied that therapists coerce clients. But the facts remain. Some do and some don't. If the most popular survivor books on the market reflect the beliefs common in the field, the problem is pronounced and cannot be denied.

During the course of my research, several therapists suggested books that they said were "very good" and " educational," in addition to *The Courage to Heal* and *Secret Survivors*, which I had asked about in the structured interview. Books recommended by the therapists (to clients and as educational tools for my reference) included *Repressed Memories* by Renee Fredrickson; *Satan's Children* and *Divided Minds*, both by Robert S. Mayer; *Satan's Underground*, a discredited book about "one woman's escape from satanic cults"; and *Michelle Remembers*, another discredited account of a therapist "discovering" horrendous repressed satanic cult memories of murder and mayhem in a client's subconscious mind. In *Michelle Remembers*, Michelle Smith and Dr. Lawrence Pazder decide from the beginning, before Michelle actually "remembers" anything, to videotape all Michelle's sessions. Soon Michelle is violently "abreacting" being raped by the devil, murdering babies, eating human flesh and so on.

Although claiming that videotapes are "documentation" of the truth of hypnotic images (and videotaping is becoming a norm among the writers of survivor manifestoes and among satanic abuse therapists), this is not normal therapeutic protocol. Videotaping is usually only used when children are involved in divorce cases in which abuse has been alleged. There is a dual-purpose for this: to show that the children were not led or coerced, and to avoid making children testify in court.

Videotaping therapy sessions and calling the tapes "documentation" is particularly suspicious since all the most famous "survivors" have claimed they *did not know* they had multiple personalities, or cult or incest "memories" until they came into counseling with unrelated conflicts or "suspicions" that something was wrong with them. A client entering therapy with suspicions should alert any well-trained therapist to the possibility that they may be dealing with a histrionic personality or a highly suggestible person badly in need of attention, and a way to meet ego needs and needs for recognition.

In cases where client and therapist serendipitously "document" the histrionics through video and audio tape, the public often accepts the manufactured documentation as evidence that the events actually occurred. The rationale for taping therapy sessions is that survivors do this to help others know are not alone. This sounds very humanitarian, but no ethical therapist would place a client at risk in this manner, either emotionally or physically.

The humanitarian rationale was also used by Truddi Chase, who collaborated with her therapist in the late 1970s in constructing 92 distinct personalities under hypnosis and on tape. She later wrote a book called *When Rabbit Howls*. "Rabbit" is said to be one of Chase's "alter personalities." To millions of TV viewers, Oprah Winfrey proclaimed Chase's personalities "documented" because there are tapes of Truddi Chase being coaxed through the construction process.

In the single case study books—*Michelle Remembers, When Rabbit Howls,* and *Lessons in Evil, Lessons from the Light*—the therapists presented video or audiotaped sessions as documentation. This is not documentation. It is nothing more than a narrative account, a story told under hypnosis or a calculated fabrication. Documentation would include past medical records and school records corroborating abuse in a concrete manner. These records would not imply abuse, they would substantiate abuse. Often, lowered grades during a semester or a visit to a doctor are cited as proof because it occurred during the time frame of abuse reported by the client. Documentation would be accurate police records of missing persons and excavated graves or disposal sites yielding evidence of missing persons who have allegedly been murdered.

Documentation would be copies of these videotapes and photographs Satanists are supposedly always taking, with the accuser as a child and the grandparents or parents wielding knives, sacrificing infants or animals, or tending the hundreds of snakes they supposedly keep for rituals. Instead, what are shown are pictures of the family in Halloween costumes, and pictures in which the accuser looked "sad" or was wearing an overcoat (supposedly to disguise a pregnancy).

Documentation is not the inconclusive results of a gynecological exam in which the doctor will not completely rule out sexual abuse, abortions or a live birth, but cannot substantiate them either. Documentation is not a few scars on the body and stories to go with the scars. Nor is it consistency in the client's story with other such stories, or internal consistency to the stories over time. Documentation is not similarities in the client's accounts to historical accounts of satanic cult rituals. There are libraries containing this kind of historical information in every town, and urban legends circulate in every town. Documentation is not the actual existence of places clients remember such as churches, graveyards and mortuaries. These too are in every town. Teenagers are known for what is known as legend tripping, or flirting with the supernatural. They gather in graveyards or remote places to drink or use drugs and tell scary stories and often construct altars or various crude monuments to their adventures. This is not proof of criminal Satanism.

High hypnotizability (and trained suggestibility) is also associated with imagination and emotional expression. All hypnotizable subjects, but particularly highly hypnotizable subjects, are also likely to undergo dissociation and experience various dissociative phenomena, one of the most dramatic being trance writing, in which the individual is not consciously aware of the thoughts that are expressed in trance. Therapists may interpret this as proof of MPD and convince the client of this as well. The use of trance writing is becoming increasingly common and is used by some therapists as a tool to activate cognitive dissonance. When clients deny or doubt images constructed in trance, they are presented with evidence in their own handwriting and then aggressively questioned about why they would lie, or asked directly if they did lie. Confabulation is not lying, and images constructed in trance and under sodium amytal are not lies. Both the processes of confabulation and the mental state of trance more closely resemble the dream state, especially the partially self-directed dream state.

The client's numerous somatic symptoms, nightmares or irrational fears are not proof of repressed memories of sexual abuse or Satanism. There are numerous somatoform disorders, mood disorders and factitious disorders, aside from the mundane symptoms of anxiety and physical aches and pains people feel, which are found on the laundry lists of recovery and survivor psychologists. In fact, with the exception of the client breathing on a daily basis, everything else is a symptom of repressed memories.

Anecdotal corroborating accounts from a relative or a story that retrospectively makes sense because it demystifies a family secret is not proof. It is not to be either dismissed nor accepted as empirical evidence. It is to be viewed as part of the narrative history of the client and if further corroboration is sought, such leads should be followed up.

Seeking corroborating evidence does not have to be a part of therapy, as long as the therapist is clear about the role of therapy as a means of allowing the client to develop a narrative history and gain greater insight into the self and personal motivations through this process. However, one of the latest trends in some factions of the therapeutic community seems to be to prove that the family is deeply pathological, justifying the premise that criminal satanists have infiltrated every level of society.

The Persuasive Smokescreen of Soft Authoritarianism

Another aspect of a persuasion tactic used within recovery and survivor psychology is the soft authoritarianism discussed by Wendy Kaminer in her commentary on the recovery movement and other self-help fads and fashions, *I'm Dysfunctional, You're Dysfunctional*. Kaminer observes that recovery authors make a pretense of free choice and egalitarianism, most claiming to be recovering addicts themselves and routinely disclaiming their own dogma. Yet she notes that while most of these authors deny being experts, they carefully list their degrees and titles behind their names and demonstrate marked propensities for making extremely dogmatic pronouncements.

John Bradshaw's writing perhaps epitomizes the practice of overgeneralization, despite his own admonishments against "toxic shame's grandiosity" and the damages of "all or nothing" maxims. He practically exudes dogmatism and self-justification with the pronouncements of recovery laws such as: "For a shame-based person, 'spiritual awakening' is impossible until the externalization work is done. Without such work, our ego-self remains ruptured and alienated"; "Spirituality is a basic human need"; "We must let go in order to grow"; and "To meditate well you must be willing to give up ego control." In the appendix of *Healing the Shame that Binds You*, Bradshaw concludes with a "Note to Psychotherapists":

> Finally, I would offer a word to those clinicians who wince at the word "spiritual." The 12-step programs have had incomparable success in healing addictions. The 12th step makes it crystal clear that one has not healed his addiction until he has had a "spiritual awakening." The millions of recovering addicts using that step are raw data enough to compel any scientist worth his salt to investigate spirituality. Toxic shame is spiritual bankruptcy in the sense I've defined. Healing this shame requires spiritual awakening in the sense I've defined.

The verdict has been delivered. Toxic shame has been defined, the only way to recovery has been made crystal clear and *scientists* should be investigating spirituality. However, the burden of proof lies with those making such claims, not with those who are skeptical of pat theories about the nature of addiction, recovery and the efficacy of treatment by the 12 steps, self-exposure and formal or informal therapy.

There is no pretense of soft authoritarianism among medieval psychologists. They are uncompromisingly authoritarian because they *know* the truth. The following quote is an example of "the truth" according to Christian psychologist James Friesen:

> The time has come for cultists to face the fact that the tide is turning. It is no longer safe for cultists. . . . It will not be safe for them to face God when they die. God is in charge, but their "master" is the prince of lies. If they repent, it is not too late. If they don't their fate is sealed. They will not be awarded a cooler place in hell, as has been promised to them, for their obedience to Satan.

Women as Primary Targets of Recovery Culture Ideologies, Survivor Psychology and Medieval Psychology

It does not seem probable that more than half of all women do not remember their own victimization, and it is cause for skepticism and concern that current research (including my own) suggests that 90 percent of the individuals recovering memories in therapy are women. Even more alarming are the numbers of MPDs and demonic possessions reportedly manifesting among a predominantly female client population in "Christ-centered" counseling programs. This rate of memory recovery and the manifestations of formerly rare psychological aberrations appearing in women appears to be affected by the focuses of recovery psychology, survivor psychology and medieval psychology. The literature, workshops, survivors groups and therapeutic modalities are largely aimed at a female audience.

Women represent the overwhelming majority of MPDs and satanic ritual abuse (SRA) case studies that appear in the survivor literature.

It would seem that if intergenerational satanic cults were operating within our family systems, educational and religious institutions and daycare centers, males would be recovering traumatic memories with the same frequency as females. However, males represent only a fraction of the individuals reportedly recovering any kind of traumatic memories in therapy.

There are several survivor logic rationales for this discrepancy too. One example is the "macho" theory that claims males will not come forward if they have been sexually abused. Yet choosing to conceal an assault for fear of public shame and the fear of not being believed is not the same as the total amnesia survivor therapists believe happens to female victims.

Another example of a survivor logic theory that explains why men are not unearthing satanic ritual abuse memories is the male dominance theory. It is claimed that males remain in the cults, and pass dominance down through their sons, who control and conceal cult activity. These same parents manipulate and mutilate their daughters and their prospective grandchildren by infant sacrifice in cult rituals. Then these daughters somehow drift away from the cults. They go to school, have careers, marry, have children that are not sacrificed, and even carry on relatively normal relations with their families—until they enter therapy. The families often support the therapy, even pay for it, yet they are supposed to be still-active cult members. None of this makes any sense. If life has no value to Satanists, why do they let alleged breeders live, drift away from the cult and carry on in society? It would be much more efficient for criminal Satanists to sacrifice all women used by the cult for sexual perversion and breeding purposes. In the male dominance theory, women are expendable anyway. Women are only involved because they supply their children; female children are only involved because they are used in cult rituals. Therefore, if a female breeder wore out her usefulness, and eradicating evidence is so essential to the secrecy of criminal Satanists, why would all these women be free agents with time, access and money to go into therapy? Many alleged breeders claim to have left the cult in their teens, yet this makes no sense either. A teenaged girl certainly has not surpassed her productive years.

The overriding reason that women are over-represented as alleged survivors could well be that the ideology of sexual abuse/incest syndromes is aimed at women. They may be powerfully influenced by these ideologies prior to entering therapy. Other influences may include (but are by no means limited to) the following factors:

1. The rapid growth of the recovery culture in which the majority of the "symptoms" of "codependence" or dysfunctionality are traditionally "feminine" roles or traits.

2. The resurrection of Freudian methods of psychoanalysis without traditional psychoanalytic training, and/or Freudianism used in a an unorthodox and aggressive manner by counselors with ideological agendas.

3. The unprecedented growth of Alcoholics Anonymous in the 1980s together with AA's notions of rampant pathology and "spiritual diseases" contributed to the corresponding development of survivor psychology without research support.

4. Widespread use of treatment modalities identified as "fringe or borderline" and "invasive and aggressive," which may iatrogenically produce memories or induce belief in sexual and incestuous victimization in the absence of memories.

5. The sudden growth of satanic ritual abuse and MPD seminars, and "Christ-centered" counseling programs.

Treasured Notions of Psychotherapy vs Interdisciplinary Approaches to Understanding Human Behavior

Two of the most treasured and persistent notions of psychotherapy are the long-term negative effects of childhood trauma and the "cycle of abuse," or "cycle of violence" theories in which the abused invariably abuse their own children or become offenders in some other context.

These notions were routinely questioned by philosophers throughout the ages and the arguments continued among psychologists, religionists, scientists and geneticists. Although we are currently seeing a resurgence in demonology theories, since the Dark Ages the theories of human behavior have developed primarily through three schools of thought: biological, psychosocial and sociocultural viewpoints. The interdisciplinary approach is currently considered essential to the study and understanding of human behavior.

Among academically and scientifically responsible social scientists, the current and prevailing theory of causation for various forms of abnormal behavior or maladjustment patterns proposes a "feedback and circularity" cycle which takes in primary, predisposing, precipitating and reinforcing causes.

Primary causes include biological disorders, which are not always sufficient to cause abnormality. A predisposing cause is one that precedes the appearance of a problem. A precipitating cause is a stressor that bears too heavily on an already stressed organism and triggers disorders. Reinforcing causes include conditions that maintain maladaptive behavior such as social reinforcements and psychological or monetary rewards. In any case, a primary cause may be unknown or absent, but two or more of the factors in the feedback and circularity causal pattern cycle may be sufficient to produce and maintain maladjustment.

Exceptions to the pressures of the causal pattern have

always been great human interest stories, even though they have not been discussed in terms of resisting the causal pattern of maladjustment and abnormality. From Norman Vincent Peale to Nathaniel Branden, the concept that people can and do rise above the worst of circumstances involving biological handicaps or abnormalities, tragic or severely abusive childhoods, extreme hardships, mammoth failures and tremendous pressures have been grist for the inspirational philosophy mill. From the narrative histories given by prominent media stars, to research following severely abused children and children of alcoholics into adulthood, the pattern of overcoming great hardships or patterns learned in childhood is far more commonplace than repeating trauma. Clearly, single-cause, one dimensional theories lead away from the facts.

Resiliency as Opposed to Pathology

In spite of the propensity in the sexual abuse recovery field to expound upon the long-term effects of child abuse, there have been few long-term follow-up studies to support this theory. The Martin and Elmer study describes the adult functioning of a group of 19 individuals who had sustained multiple bone lesions from severe battery as children. The overall study findings indicated no simple cause and effect relationship between early trauma and adult functioning. The subjects showed average self-esteem scores and as a group showed no consistent evidence of emotional problems. These findings do not appear to distinguish this severely abused population from any randomly chosen population.

In Widom's study of the "cycle of violence" and "intergenerational transmission of violence," the researcher states that the two notions have become "the premier developmental hypotheses in the field of abuse and neglect." Widom points out that people tend to have strong feelings on these topics, but this should not preclude awareness of the methodological difficulties of this type of research and the unresolved questions.

Methodological weaknesses of studies dealing with the presumed relationship between childhood trauma, repetition of abuse and adult dysfunctions include "overdependence on self-report and retrospective data, inadequate documentation of childhood abuse and neglect, and infrequent use of baseline data from control groups."

In a comprehensive review of the literature, Widom cites Kauf and Ziglcr, who conclude that "the unqualified acceptance of the intergenerational transmission hypothesis from abuse as a child to becoming an abusive parent is unfounded."

A related repetition/compulsion theory is that abused and neglected children are more likely to become criminals, and that the majority of criminals were abused as children. This theory was tested in the Femina, Yeager and Lewis study on child abuse as a predisposing factor to criminality. The authors state, "Although much of the research on adult violence and victimization relies on retrospective reporting of abuse, remarkably little is known about the validity of such information."

Sixty-nine subjects who had been incarcerated as delinquents were given follow-up interviews in the Femina study. Twenty-six gave reports that were discrepant with their adolescent responses. The researchers concluded that former delinquents tend to deny or minimize serious childhood abuse. They cite the Feldman, Pincus, Jackson and Bard study and the Feldman, Lewis and Mallouh study, which showed that condemned individuals tend to deny or minimize childhood abuse. This was an unexpected result, given the researchers' hypotheses that such individuals would be more likely to exaggerate abuse to get sympathy. There are alternative hypothetical options. For instance, some adolescents may be likely to perceive parental discipline as unnecessarily punitive and call it "abuse." It may also be that adult convicts are accurately reporting, and in fact, child abuse is not a predisposing factor in adult criminality in and of itself. Other primary, reinforcing and predisposing causes may need to be present in combination with reports of child abuse among criminals to conclude that child abuse may have been one of many interacting factors.

Other researchers have been forced to take note of the number of children who do surprisingly well despite maltreatment. Researchers Patricia Mrazek and David Mrazek have focused their efforts on the study of what protective factors contribute to the resilience of abused children. In their study, "Resilience in Child Maltreatment Victims: A Conceptual Exploration," the researchers hypothesized 12 factors that foster resilience and abort maladaptive outcomes. These factors are:

> 1) rapid responsivity to danger; 2) precocious maturity; 3) dissociation of affect; 4) information seeking; 5) formation and utilization of relationships for survival; 6) positive projective anticipation; 7) decisive risk taking; 8) the conviction of being loved; 9) idealization of aggressor's competence; 10) cognitive restructuring of painful experiences; 11) altruism; 12) optimism and hope.

Some of the above protective elements of resilience are disease symptoms in recovery and survivor psychology, and it is believed by survivor psychologists that these functional and protective skills should be aggressively broken down and remolded.

Step one is to affirm what the client or potential convert often proudly reports as lessons or skills learned in childhood as survival skills. Then the age-inappropriate indoctrination begins along with labeling and role assignments, such as "hero, lost child, mascot." Then clients or potential converts are told the behaviors and beliefs that saved them in the past are now "killing them." In effect, the client or potential convert must repent, reframe and replace working survival skills with recovery or survivor ideology.

The lack of research for the theories of recovery, survivor and medieval psychologists is often matched by the lack of objectivity shown by the few who do research and obtain unexpected outcomes. The reversible quality of the theories of recovery/survivor psychology is illustrated in a study by Janet Woititz (who popularized the term "adult children of alcoholics"), which was designed to measure the self-esteem of children of alcoholics who attended Alateen and those who did not.

The expected outcome was that Alateens would show higher self-esteem scores. When the opposite result was found, the researcher concluded that the non-participants were in denial, which accounted for the higher self-esteem found in this group. Stanton Peele, in *Diseasing of America: Addiction Treatment Out of Control,* captures this twist of logic in the following remark:

> According to Woititz, it only seems that children of alcoholics have higher self-esteem when they don't enter treatment, but they are actually *denying* their low self-esteem. Woititz is confident, however, that the children will be better off when this artificial self-esteem is stripped away.

The concept of denial serves a multitude of functions in recovery/survivor psychological systems, not the least of which is to categorically deny the intrusion of reality into their ideologies.

Chapter Six

How to Avoid Thinking:
Survivor Logic

*Acceptance of the faulty explanation
is never justifiable on political or moral
grounds. . . . no claim of a putative social
or political consequence because of the
acceptance of a correct explanation ever
justifies rejection of that explanation.*

—Steven Goldberg
When Wish Replaces Thought

The entire system of survivor psychology and recovery culture psychology is built on "true believer" logic. True believer logic is defined by Steven Goldberg, author of *When Wish Replaces Thought*, as a system of fallacious and subjective arguments which "have no logical consistency, are discordant with the empirical evidence, and either fail to explain that which they claim to explain or offer explanations of that which does not exist." This is the definition I have used for survivor logic as well.

The basic principles of survivor logic are outlined below. Examples will follow the list.

Principle 1—*Personalize the issues.*

The arguments are based on emotionally charged statements and "I messages."

Principle 2— *The opposing argument becomes the proof.*

Hard evidence in support of the opposing viewpoint, or the lack of evidence for the belief is used as "evidence" and strengthens beliefs instead of challenging them.

Principle 3—*When confronted with logical discrepancies, revert to God, society or morality.*

When the evidence is stacked against the beliefs and the true believer is backed into a corner, they retreat behind their preferred social control modality—religion, political rhetoric and moral crusade monologues.

Principle 4— *When in doubt, abort further interaction or exploration of the issues by playing "Ain't it Awful" games while* *stepping up the intensity.*

When the true believer is backed into a corner, he or she often reverts to a favorite ideological or abortive interaction game (or plays all of them sequentially): God's Will; The Oppressor and the Oppressed; The Power of Evil and What Happens When Good People Do Nothing; Social Decline and Moral Decay; This Hurts Me as Much as It Hurts You; I Know This Is Hard to Believe—I Used to Be a Skeptic Too!; The Experts Know Best; Suicide; Revictimization; No Motive; and I'm Only Trying to Help.

Principle 5— *When all else fails, bring up denial and conspiracy theories.*

Constructing Evidence Using the
Survivor Logic Formula

One of latest additions to the genre of books written by therapists who help clients dig up pornographic, criminal and sadistic "memories" through hypnosis is Gail Feldman's *Lessons in Evil, Lessons From the Light: A True Story of Satanic Abuse and Spiritual Healing.* Like the rest of the most famous case studies, Feldman's client "Barbara" knew nothing about her decade of "satanic ritual abuse" or that her mother, grandmother, grandfather and extended family members sustained intergenerational involvement with satanic cults (Game: No Motive). They were strict fundamentalist Christians by day and depraved blood cult members by night (Principle 2—The opposing argument or evidence becomes the proof).

Barbara has been in therapy before but has been unable to get better. Feldman describes her as "impeccably dressed, well-educated, employed and accomplished." Yet she hates sex, cannot socialize, despises her body, cannot shop or spend money, and is irrationally angry at her seven-year-old daughter. In addition, Barbara is suicidal, has horrible nightmares, claims no self-esteem and has fantasies about cutting herself open and "pulling her insides out." In spite of all these adjustment problems, compulsive thoughts and affective disorders, Feldman claims Barbara is "the most stable person I have ever known." The description of Barbara's emotional adjustment and the illogical conclusion that this woman is stable and therefore not suffering from other delusions or personality problems is based on Principle 2—the opposing argument or evidence becomes the proof.

Feldman reports that Barbara came to her because Barbara had heard she uses hypnosis. They begin hypnotic regressions almost immediately, with Dr. Feldman discovering that Barbara is a good subject, and according to the eye roll test, is highly hypnotizable (Principle 2—instead of exercising caution because of the client's suggestibility, this is presented enthusiastically as a good sign to go ahead).

The eye roll test is considered a fairly stable predictor of hypnotizability, with only around 10 percent of the population highly hypnotizable and able to roll the eyes back while still open and reveal white sclera completely as Barbara can do. Although the majority of highly hypnotizable people are psychologically normal, hypnotizability can be associated with certain symptomatology that includes "a tendency to compulsively comply with others, a nonrational inner sense of inferiority, and a variety of spontaneous dissociative and conversion symptoms." When Feldman puts Barbara in a trance, she immediately begins recalling murders, beginning with the killing of her pet cat, after which Barbara is forced to drink the blood and eat part of the heart. Barbara becomes worse and worse, and the memories become increasingly bizarre. None of these signs cause the doctor to exercise caution.

Feldman reports her increasingly tense relationship with her husband as a result of her work with Barbara (Game:

This Hurts Me as Much as It Hurts You). Mr. Feldman is skeptical and becomes angry that his wife must tell him the gory details of Barbara's sessions. He questions Barbara's sanity and wonders why these survivors seem to find his wife so regularly. This angers Dr. Feldman, who blows up at her husband and blames the history of male dominance and sexual abuse on male insensitivity. If not for women infiltrating the mental health profession, she claims women would be subjected to 75 more years of non-belief (Game: The Oppressor and the Oppressed).

Dr. Feldman spends many pages trying to convince the reader that she was unprepared for Barbara's case (Games: This Hurts Me as Much as It Hurts You, and I Know This Is Hard to Believe). In fact, Feldman's "education" in satanic ritual abuse begins formally when Barbara gives her a copy of *Michelle Remembers*, the 1980 forerunner of the popular crypto-pedophilic genre of SRA books currently polluting the pop psychology market (Game: I Know This Is Hard to Believe—I Used to Be a Skeptic Too!).

Feldman's book follows the factoid manifesto formula to the letter: contrived skepticism; increasing conversion to a belief in both evil and Christianity; the use of other survivors manifestoes as proof; and the construction of evidence via audio tapes and other documentation that only shows that accusations have been made.

The foreword to Feldman's book is written by Carl Raschke, a professor of religious studies at the University of Denver. Raschke gives his opinions and justifications for why the account given by Feldman and her client should be considered true, and why other accounts should be considered true if they follow a consistent pattern.

1. The complete lack of evidence for Barbara's accounts and other such accountings is actually *proof* because it is consistent with cult programming, which ensures that survivors will not be able to produce evidence (Principle 2—

the opposing argument or evidence becomes the proof).

2. Raschke claims that the painstaking clinical process by which Feldman documents her client's sessions are not only proof that she did not lead her client, it is also proof of a broader variety (Game: The Experts Know Best). Feldman's documentation of Barbara's memories makes it possible that "the reader can easily see that the fashionable accusation that survivors are simply telling tales in order to 'please the therapist' has no grounding." First of all, the oversimplified notion that the only criticism of bad therapy is that eager-to-please clients tell tales, addresses the least likely scenario of all. The dynamics of influence, suggestibility, psychological and physiological disorders are far more complicated than that. How one therapist's clinical process with one client generalizes to negate all the current criticisms of exploitive therapeutic techniques based on what is known about suggestion, interpersonal cuing, social psychology and the dynamics of influence, is incomprehensible logic. If the process as written in Feldman's book is an accurate accounting of her sessions with Barbara, Feldman has documented the contamination process quite adequately. There is certainly no evidence of a painstaking clinical process, which would involve much more than audio taping a client under hypnosis and keeping case notes.

3. The patient is skeptical of her own memories. The con job to sell clients on repressed memories always includes a section on disbelief and denial. (Game: I Know This Is Hard to Believe). Yet, according to Raschke this is not a trait usually found among dissociative patients who would simply be confabulating. If skepticism is not characteristic of true survivors, then every single survivor book on the market is *wrong* about its criteria for judging the veracity of repressed memories. Fredrickson says: "Crippling disbelief is the hallmark of repressed memories." Bass and Davis

claim: "Believing doesn't usually happen all at once—it's a gradual awakening." Lauren Stratford, author of *Satan's Underground*, says: "The way I was raised was so ugly and traumatic that for many years of my adult life the memories haunted me day and night, I refused to accept them as reality, let alone reveal them to anyone else." James Friesen, satanic ritual abuse counselor, claims: "It takes time for most people to trust a therapist enough to open up about deep issues. Considering how many people have failed the client, we can understand that it can take a lot of time for him or her to trust enough to accept this particular diagnosis."

4. Feldman is a "highly respected" hypnotherapist, therefore she understands the "potentialities" of "her art" which should "leave far less doubt in the readers mind" (Game: The Expert Knows Best).

5. The survivor recalls "real places" that are "identifiable." This is a good one. Totally meaningless in terms of what is true or untrue.

6. The survivor's memories are consistent with what "is known from other sources about the occult." This is not proof. In fact, if anything it implies contamination (Principle 2—the opposing argument or evidence becomes the proof).

Survivor Therapists and the Search for Repressed Memories

The assumption that clients are severely or noticeably damaged by what they do not remember was common among the mental health practitioners in my 1992 survey. Ninety-nine percent of the therapists answered "yes" or "sometimes" to the question, "Do you work with clients who display the symptomatology of sexual abuse and incest survivors but have no memories?" All but one in the random sample believed that clients displayed a clear symptomatology that indicated repressed memories. This means that attentional biases, selective reinforcement of symptoms and survivor psychology logic are more common than the counseling community generally likes to admit.

When I say random sample, I mean that after I established the interview process in the therapeutic community, I simply asked for referrals to other therapists specializing in sexual abuse recovery. This does not indicate that the beliefs expressed by the therapists in the sample generalize to all therapists, or even to all therapists claiming to specialize in sexual abuse issues. I had no control over who was going to call me back, and I did not pursue some leads that would have badly skewed the data, such as a "past life" regressionist claiming to be an expert in repressed sexual abuse. Even so, it was surprisingly easy to find therapists practicing aggressive therapeutic modalities and espousing completely subjective and unscientific beliefs about repression, memory storage and retrieval. If these modalities and beliefs are so uncommon, why are such therapists so easy to find, and why are the survivor books full of these notions and practices?

According to Robert Mayer, it is essential to dig up "repressed memories" in troubled clients. Mayer claims it is the "only way to truly free them." But Mayer relies on the power of the situation, using a combination of quasi-psychological mumbo-jumbo, reinforcing the "sick" role of the patient and authoritatively wielding the power vested in therapists. According to Mayer:

> The treatment of multiple personality disorder is simple, at least theoretically. The therapist helps the patient pry open the lid of the psychic container and the memory of the traumatic episode is freed, becoming disarmed in the process. In practice, though, treat-

ing multiples is a long and difficult process. After all, patients have gone to great lengths to forget these episodes, and now the therapist must not only make them remember, but actually sense and feel and reexperience the traumas, for that is the only way to truly free them. This means I have to take patients on a guided trip back to the hell of their childhoods.

Mayer's convictions are shared by satanic abuse counselor James Friesen, author of *Uncovering the Mystery of MPD: Its Shocking Origins, Its Surprising Cure.* Friesen relates what he says to clients about the "therapeutic journey," using similar vivid imagery to describe the "festering" of "traumatic memories" and to explain to the confused client how such memories could exist without his or her knowledge. The theory is also designed to justify the aggressive modalities used to "uncover" the "repressed memories":

> God has created us with remarkable ways of protecting ourselves from being bombarded by traumatic memories. The mind works very hard to hide them and therapy often requires people to work just as hard to recover them. . . . Why do the memories need to be recovered? Because their wounds ooze into daily life as long as they remain hidden and unhealed. The frustrating feelings in your current life are almost certainly fed by hidden pain from your past.

Survivor therapist Renee Fredrickson explains the need for aggressive methods of memory construction or the "active search for your hidden past," and also manages to work in soft-sell tactics in the following passage:

> Repressed memories are pieces of your past that have become a mystery. They stalk your unconscious and

hamper your life with their aftermath. They will tell you a story if you only know how to listen to them, and the story will help you make sense of your life and your pain. As the story unfolds, you wonder if your mind has played a trick on you, causing you to make up strange, sad, and sometimes horrifying tales of abuse.

Your mind has played a trick on you, but it is a trick to help you rather than hurt you. . . . your wonderful, powerful mind hid some or all of the abuse from you until you were strong enough to face it.

Your repressed memories were held in storage not only for your readiness to deal with them, but also for society's readiness to deal with them.

It is uncanny how survivor psychologists manage to follow the same rationale and use a variation of the same soft-sell script—and yet each one of them uses their own preferred social control modality or ideology to hammer home the rationale and the implied rewards of memory work. Friesen blames repressed memories on how God created the mind to work (Principle 3—when confronted with logical discrepancies, revert to God, society or morality). Like all survivor psychologists who use God or religious ideology as a supporting theory, Friesen is enthusiastic about repression and calls it "remarkable." Mayer vacillates between a chummy, self-deprecating style and then hides behind authoritative jargon and presents himself as a reluctant healer.

Fredrickson cleverly uses society as an instrument of automatic memory repression, stating that memories are "held in storage" for when the individual is ready, and when society is ready. This implies a ready-made rationalization for why repressed memories have suddenly become a huge industry and *millions* of people have them.

Fredrickson's social oppression theory also provides an implied built-in warning: Anyone who challenges Fredrickson's ideology is an oppressor (Principle 3).

Survivor psychologists who prefer to use Principle 3 and use the games The Oppressor and the Oppressed and Moral Decline and Decay tend to cite the theories of Freudian-oriented psychoanalyst Alice Miller. Miller's theories have been widely used as a foundation for recovery culture and survivor psychology. Miller tends toward traditional psychoanalytic theory and the belief that early trauma sets up repetition/compulsion cycles. Alice Miller's book, *For Your Own Good: Hidden Cruelty in Child-Rearing and the Roots of Violence*, contains the "Poisonous Pedagogy," which are theoretically the soul-murdering rules by which soul-murdered parents unconsciously soul-murder their own children. The book also includes Miller's list of false beliefs transmitted in family systems. These beliefs are thought to contribute to the repetition/compulsion cycle of soul-murdering children.

Both of these manifestoes were popularized in Bradshaw's 1987 book, *Bradshaw On: The Family*. Bradshaw expounded at length on the effects of the Poisonous Pedagogy. According to Miller, the pedagogy ensures that soul murder takes place before children know what happened, and consequently they will be compelled to unconsciously repeat this pattern with their own children. This amnesiac, repetition/compulsion theory adapts well to fear-based appeals from the social consciousness and political sales model.

Survivor Logic and the Sale of Dissociative Disorders

The three predominant survivor logic themes and sales tactics evident in the works of survivor psychologists dealing with the issues of dissociative disorders are all based on Principle 2 of survivor logic—*the opposing argument or evi-*

142

dence becomes the proof. The marketing of dissociative disorders will be covered under the following subheadings:
1. The sales and promotion of the MPD hypothesis.
2. Sexual abuse, repressed memories, MPD and Satanism—the dynamics preceding their appearance and the rationales for lack of evidence.
3. The misdiagnosed schizophrenic hypothesis and the assumption that delusional accounts are true because they are similar.
4. Sexual abuse, Satanism, schizophrenia and survivor logic.
5. Denial and conspiracy theories.

The Sales and Promotion of the MPD Hypothesis

Multiple personality disorder (MPD) is currently the trendy disease in the recovery culture and is the latest pop and pulp psychology craze. The October 1993 issue of *Changes* magazine, a recovery culture publication, included an article on MPD by C.W. Duncan, Ph.D., author of *The Fractured Mirror: Healing Multiple Personality Disorder.* Duncan promises to "give you the facts, the good and the bad, so you can judge for yourself whether or not you have MPD. If you come to agree with your tentative diagnosis, the book will help you prepare for successful therapy." Duncan also stresses the difficulty of MPD psychotherapy, but claims "no psychotherapy promises as successful an outcome, if you truly commit to it." Duncan even has a seven point laundry list entitled "Are You a Multiple?" and claims experts endorse these as symptoms.

The article is a typical example of a factoid manifesto. Duncan uses all the tricks of the trade common among survivor psychologists: soft authoritarianism; implied credibility; unnamed sources; a chummy, condescending writing style; contrived skepticism; built-in incentives to sell the disease and the therapy; a laundry list; and even an opening argument designed to make you think you already thought you were an MPD in the first place.

Consider the following scenario that Duncan creates in the opening page of the article:

> One of your friends in the incest survivors group is MPD, but it never occurred to you that you might be one too, or has it? "Possibly," you thought, but quickly dismissed it as an unlikely notion. Oh, you had heard about MPD from books, movies, TV soaps and talk shows. "But surely, I am not like them." You buried the hunch deep inside until now. "The doctor said that I may have MPD." "No, I don't!" "Yes, I do!" "That's ridiculous!" "No, it isn't!" The internal argument continued, but the question hovered in the air like a stubborn mosquito.

It is obvious that the recovery culture is hoping to mine this revamped version of an old pre-Freudian psychological theory now that other recovery culture disease processes are tapped out and boring. Duncan even whips up a little competitive spirit, bringing up a friend from your incest survivors group that "has MPD." It's just not trendy anymore to go to your incest survivors group with nothing more serious than love addiction or an eating disorder.

All the principles of survivor logic show up in Duncan's brief advertisement cleverly disguised as an informative article. Principle 2—the opposing argument or evidence becomes the proof—is Duncan's predominant technique. Under the subtitle "Separating the Hype from Reality," Duncan repackages the hype with Ain't It Awful and Revictimization games. He talks about the lurid tabloids and talk shows that have seemingly exploited a serious mental health issue, yet then he leaps inside the heads of the skeptics and the poor performing MPDs who must manifest their "alters" on television to prove they are not faking. "Man alive!" thinks Duncan's prototypical skeptic, "Think what I could get away with by saying my alter did it." Meanwhile, the multiple being interviewed and interrogated is thinking, "These people have no idea. They think I'm putting all this on."

Then we are asked to imagine *her* humiliation when she realizes she has been exploited and laughed at. "It feels like abuse all over again," Duncan informs us (Game: Revictimization). More great revelations: "Audiences love sensationalism, and television gives them what they want to see: confused and frightened individuals suffering from an exotic malady." The implication is that what we are seeing on TV and reading in the tabloids is true after all. It is just exploitation of "the truth."

Duncan quickly covers the objections to the gross over-diagnosis of MPD in today's pulp psychology circles. MPD is not a new disorder. It's 100 years old, and the psychological community *still* won't accept MPD as a valid diagnosis. They "refuse to diagnose it, and subsequently fail to treat it correctly," Duncan petulantly asserts (Game: The Oppressor and the Oppressed). It's not that the mental health community just doesn't want to *let* MPD be a valid diagnosis, it's that the research and scientific factions of the psychological community *cannot* find evidence that the appearance of MPD is uncomplicated by attentional biases from therapists. Until very recently, MPD was rare and did not emerge unless it was in a therapeutic situation. However, with Duncan's self-help book and his affirmation that "you can judge for yourself whether or not you have MPD," we will probably see numerous self-diagnosed cases on talk shows and in the tabloids.

That MPD generally appears after six or seven years in therapy, and that the same client has been previously diagnosed with everything from schizophrenia to PMS is

Duncan's "proof" of the tragic misdiagnosis of MPD (Principle 2—the opposing argument becomes the evidence). Duncan is incredulous that the "remarkable" case of Eve did not convince the psychological community that MPD was real once and for all. "One shudders to think how many individuals were mistakenly diagnosed and 'treated' during the intervening years." The "mistaken diagnosis" theory is a frequent survivor logic justification for why this syndrome has suddenly exploded and is intended to create a little false history that lends credibility and negates opposing evidence.

True to the principles of survivor logic, the syndrome is presented as credible because it appears after lengthy therapy. Yet in the responsible mental health community, even the inclusion of MPD in the *Diagnostic and Statistical Manual of Mental Disorders* is controversial—precisely *because* the syndrome appears most frequently after lengthy therapy that is psychoanalytical in orientation and usually includes hypnotherapy. It is the potential for contamination through the use of these techniques that make the diagnosis questionable.

One of the most interesting (and potentially persuasive) developments in the studies of individuals manifesting multiple personalities surfaced when it was found that their brain scans appeared different, and biochemical changes occurred with the manifestations of "alter" personalities. The characteristic changes such as voice pitch, mannerisms, linguistic and grammatical changes, affect, hand preferences, or speaking in a language foreign to that individual have always been observed and have been easily explained away by skeptics as faking or acting.

When biochemical changes were observed in MPD subjects, the faking or acting the role of an MPD and "hysterical conversion" theories were deflated a bit. However, recent developments in psycho-neuroimmunology have reopened those issues and raised even more questions. In the Nicholas Hall and Dennis Calandra study, "Performance-Induced Personality Transformation and Immunity," the researchers found that actors playing different roles showed different biological markers in the blood before and after various role-playing situations. Hall's previous work had showed alterations in body chemistry in patients undergoing personality changes. Hall repeated his work with actors and found similar results. Neither finding is conclusive and more research must be done to make any sort of definitive statement, but it raises some interesting questions regarding the MPD hypothesis as a relevant psychiatric disorder.

Long-term therapy and a series of therapists are common dynamics in the diagnosis of MPD and the "discovery" of repressed memories. Although MPD is currently considered grossly overdiagnosed, this has not deterred sexual abuse therapists from speculating that most MPD cases were caused by sexual abuse and that many schizophrenic patients are actually misdiagnosed sexual abuse victims who have manifested multiple personalities to protect themselves.

Sexual Abuse, Repressed Memories, MPD and Satanism—The Dynamics Preceding Their Appearance and the Rationales for Lack of Evidence

The dynamics preceding the emergence of MPD are identical to the dynamics preceding the emergence of repressed memories of incest and sexual abuse. According to Dr. Robert S. Mayer, author of *Through Divided Minds* and *Satan's Children*, a sensationalistic series of undocumented case studies, "The average patient with multiple personality disorder spends almost seven years with at least three therapists before he is correctly diagnosed."

Mayer explains how he gets his patients to "discharge trauma" through hypnosis and aggressive lines of questioning to "bring it all out of their consciousness":

> ... it can be an extraordinarily difficult process. Some-
> times, it takes a patient years to abreact a memory, if
> they ever abreact it. .... It seems unfair that to heal
> themselves, to recover from what someone else did to
> them, patients have to go through it all over again. So
> they resist.
>
> Still, I had a fair amount of success coaxing
> abreactions from people who had been referred to me.
> Afterward, I would explain to them that what they
> had just gone through amounted to a psychic opera-
> tion and that it would take a while to recover. Then I
> would send them back to their analysts for continuing
> treatment.

It seems presumptuous, to say the least, that Mayer would
assume that he is justified in "coaxing" abreactions or performing "psychic operations" on clients, then sending his
psychically wounded clients back to their analysts for continuing treatment. This aggressive method bears no relationship to currently acceptable psychoanalytic procedures
in which clients are neither coaxed or subjected to metaphorical operations through hypnotic plundering of the
mind.

According to Mayer, and many other medieval or survivor psychologists, the "memories" are supposedly deeply
repressed because of programming and mind control procedures by satanic cult members, and are constantly "reac-
tivated" by otherwise innocuous words and environmental
cues. This is a survivor logic justification to explain away
why former cult members never remember anything until
it is too late to do anything about it, and why memories
must be dredged up in aggressive therapy sessions.

If the satanic cults are so bloodthirsty and powerful, how

did all these members end up alive, alone and in analysis? If the cults have the capabilities and connections to completely eradicate evidence of murders and crimes, it would seem that no one could escape them, yet it seems that thousands are doing just that, based on the explosion of satanic abuse seminars, the literature on satanic abuse, and the many MPDs and SRAs that are currently sustaining the inpatient and outpatient economy.

One common technique of persuasion already covered at length is contrived skepticism. Rene Diamond, SRA counselor and seminar leader, good-naturedly admits that what she is about to say is "weird" and that a few years ago she wouldn't have believed it. James Friesen claims that a few years ago he would have denied the existence of satanic ritual abuse. Mayer expresses skepticism throughout both of his books, particularly at highly implausible passages. He creates little arguments he has with himself and then reports even more implausible events as if they were factual accounts (Game: I Know This Is Hard to Believe—I Used to Be a Skeptic Too).

Mayer concludes *Satan's Children* with another of his many anecdotes. He is on a fishing expedition with a friend who knows nothing of Mayer's involvement with MPDs. They stumble upon a clearing containing two "throne-like" chairs built from piles of stone and a flat stone that Mayer thinks might be an altar. The doctor's friend casually remarks that "there have been stories of devil worship around here." The book ends with Mayer staring at the scene for a few moments and following his friend back into the woods.

Mayer's writing style is extremely manipulative and he openly admits that he is coercive in uncovering repressed memories and must *make* clients remember. He talks about being gratified by being considered an expert and says that he loves dramatics as do his MPD clients. Mayer also claims to become attached to his clients' alters or other personalities. In fact, he reports grieving when they go away as a result of therapy. Mayer becomes maudlin when he talks about the pain of treating multiples. As personalities integrate, he loses friends (Game: This Hurts Me as Much as It Hurts You). Instead of a hundred fragmentary personalities that need to be integrated in therapy, Mayer claims he ends up with only one integrated, but still disturbed, individual who now must continue therapy to adjust to normalcy.

Mayer's attachment to "alters" seems to be a very misguided form of transference as well as what is called "selective reinforcement of symptoms." Rene Diamond, a self-proclaimed expert in satanic ritual abuse and MPD, also gets teary-eyed about her attachment to patients' alters and talks about how "wonderful" and "creative" MPDs are.

Mayer's anecdotes, observations and treatment methods are not supportable by scientific data. He provides no evidence, nor does he report any data on treatment outcomes. He simply claims his MPDs "get better." Mayer's treatment notions are shared by Diamond, Thompson and Friesen, who believe that clients must be guided through the "living hells" of their pasts, and also simply claim that their clients get better through long-term therapy. The notion of getting better is essentially meaningless in psychology. There are no empirical ways to measure the notion of getting better.

The "Misdiagnosed Schizophrenic" Hypothesis and the Assumption that Delusional Accounts Are True Because They Are Similar

One of the most frequent arguments in support of recovered memories and the satanic ritual abuse hypothesis is the consistency of the reports given by the psychiatric patients and alleged survivors. However, the reports are not original, remarkable or unusual. The content of therapeutically constructed mental images of satanic abuse contains common cultural archetypes of the devil or Satan, and common cultural stereotypes of satanic rituals and worship services. The rituals include chanting, infanticide, human and animal sacrifice, cannibalism, symbolic marriages and pacts with the devil, rape, forced impregnation, orgies, torture, drinking blood or urine and so on.

A number of cases of reported satanic abuse have been recanted. The reversals have occurred when patients left an institution or a therapist. They have also occurred when psychologists refused to encourage and reinforce the mental images, going against the admonition that helping professionals must always believe and affirm anything the client claims is a memory or the beginning of a memory. Other cases have been discredited through the legal system and community solidarity.

The argument that the mental health industry serves political ends has been an ongoing philosophical conflict. Thomas Szasz, a prominent voice in this wave of skepticism, has even asserted that the diagnosis of schizophrenia is a psychological dumping ground for mental aberrations or behavioral characteristics the mental health community does not understand or does not agree with. However, even if schizophrenia is not an isolated mental illness, in some cases it may describe a syndrome with common characteristics that may be partly due to the socialization that occurs in mental hospital settings, and partly due to organic impairment. In many individuals, the symptoms are controllable by anti-psychotic medications, so biochemical components or organic impairment is clearly a factor in the onset and appearance of schizophrenia. In any case, the misdiagnosed schizophrenic theory is becoming a factor in the means by which sexual abuse theorists justify the high estimates of abuse and deflect the argument that repressed abuse syndromes appeared rather suddenly, accompanying the advent of recovery and survivor psychology. The misdiagnosed schizophrenic hypothesis appears most often in conjunction with claims of satanic ritual abuse.

The rationale that the accounts of satanic ritual abuse given by psychiatric patients with severe dissociative disorders are true by virtue of the similarities in their stories seems gullible, considering the sources of the accounts and because evidence is rarely sought to substantiate the accounts. Common themes and delusions have always been characteristic of schizophrenia. Schizophrenic delusions are practically identical to the reports given by satanic abuse survivors or medieval psychologists.

The types of common themes that occur among schizophrenic patients include instructions from the devil and visitations by the devil, or on the other hand, receiving instructions from God (usually of a negative nature); hearing voices or internal conversations; preoccupation with sexual themes; believing that outer forces are controlling them or attempting to control them; "thought broadcasting," or believing their thoughts or the thoughts of others are being transmitted or received; and numerous somatic delusions such as being subjected to repeated rapes by demons, or being subjected to unnecessary and secret operations by teams of evil surgeons or alien beings. These delusions are frequently accompanied by self-mutilating behaviors, often in attempts to release demons or repel evil forces. Schizophrenics often imagine that food is poisoned or drugged, become convinced that they have been forced to consume drugs or participate in bizarre sexual acts or murders, and suffer from a variety of delusions with religious and sexual themes.

The similarities in schizophrenic delusions do not cause psychiatrists to assume that what these patients are hearing, seeing or imagining are true and actually happening, but there is a general consensus among mental health professionals that it is counterproductive to challenge a schizophrenic in the throes of a delusion. Responsible mental health professionals neither encourage nor validate delusions as a means of treatment. The preferred course is to attempt to correct a chemical imbalance if diagnosed, and not reinforce or challenge the delusion while it is active.

Sexual Abuse, Satanism, Schizophrenia and Survivor Logic

The association between the dramatic rise in reports of MPD cases and the anecdotal educational process that links satanic ritual abuse with MPD has not gone unnoticed by many psychiatrists and investigators. The belief in both syndromes, and the corresponding rise in reports, has been cultivated through the oral tradition of workshops in the therapeutic network and religious community.

The similarities in the accounts given by schizophrenic patients and those given by satanic ritual abuse survivors is evident in the reports given on the 37 patients in the Young, Sachs, Braun and Watkins study. The researchers reported claims of "forced drug usage, sexual abuse, witnessing and receiving physical abuse/torture, witnessing animal mutilation and killings, being buried alive in coffins or graves, death threats, forced witnessing and forced participation in infant sacrifice and murder of adults and children, 'marriage to Satan,' forced impregnation and sacrifice of own child, and forced cannibalism."

The symptoms of the clinical syndrome of satanic abuse included "unusual fears, survivor guilt, indoctrinated beliefs, substance abuse, severe post-traumatic stress disorder, bizarre self-abuse, sexualization of sadistic impulses, and dissociative states with satanic overtones." Other symptoms reported common to the study population were "hearing internal voices or conversations, experiencing a sense of being controlled by outer forces, and periods of amnesia." The authors of the study state, "These (symptoms) were related to the underlying dissociative disorder and were not symptoms of psychosis."

This appears to be a rather authoritative statement, given the lack of hard evidence for the accounts given by the psychiatric inpatients. The authors confirm that none of the cases were referred to law enforcement. Family members were not contacted for verification because of the patients' fears of retaliation.

The Jonker, Jonker-Bakker study is another frequently cited work in the promotion of the urban legends of the Satanism and ritual abuse rings. In May of 1987, two cases of abuse were reported in the small community of Oude Pekela in the Netherlands. Over an 18-month period, the two cases grew to 98 cases in which the children testified to being regularly abducted and forced to commit sexual acts with adults, bathed in colored water, dressed in animal costumes, smeared with feces, beaten, choked, tied to poles, photographed nude, videotaped, locked in closets or cages, witnessed infant sacrifice in a church, and suffered numerous additional abuses.

The 18-month investigation yielded no evidence, no location, no physical evidence on any of the children, with the exception of one of the first two boys. This one child experienced anal bleeding. (It was later discovered that the boy was poked with a stick by another boy.) Even so, the researchers proposed that disbelief by a large number of people had a negative effect on the children, and that children who recanted a story or admitted to making it all up may have been reacting to pressure and fear because of the effect ritualistic abuse has on children. The authors felt compelled to stress that "Interviewers of sexually abused children must not reject a child's story, no matter how impossible or bizarre it seems." The authors then suggested systematic interviews and medical exams to verify future reports of ritual abuse, which would certainly lend credibility to the charges, but if the stories must always be unchallenged, no matter how bizarre, even credible researchers may be powerless to debunk urban legends because skepticism is now considered damaging and even anti-therapeutic.

Conspiracy and Denial Theories

All the usual reasons why there is no proof of satanic activity are offered in *The Courage to Heal*—society is in denial, investigators do not document the stories because they are too unpleasant, prosecutors do not want to take cases they might lose for fear of hurting their careers, and Satanists have supernatural powers that eradicate evidence, as well as techniques of mind control that surpass any known methods.

Sandi Gallant, a law enforcement officer who conducts seminars on satanic ritual abuse and investigates cases of alleged ritualistic crime, makes the classic pitch for the "truth" of the stories in *The Courage to Heal*:

> The allegations are extremely consistent, the allegations were consistent even before there was media coverage of these cases; children don't make up stories like these, human beings may be technologically advanced but we're basically just animals; if we can imagine these things happening four or five hundred years ago, then we have to start believing they are happening today.

The logic used to insist on the veracity of the accounts is consistent with the logic of all true believers, whether the subject is UFO abductions, past life regressions, channeling or psychic healing.

It is assumed that people asking for evidence are doing so because they want to discredit the accounts, when, in fact, if Satanism or child abuse exists in the proportions claimed by survivor psychologists, evidence would provide the impetus for action (Principle 1—personalize the issues). No one, not law enforcement agencies, social institutions or concerned citizens, can effectively do anything when the "victims" presume that any form of investigation or logical questioning is "revictimization."

Media coverage was not a factor in promoting social hysterias prior to the early 1900s, and the content of various cultural myths regarding demonology are passed on by vehicles as innocent as children's fairy tales. The actual existence of demons, devil worship or witchcraft is not something historians can "imagine happening four or five hundred years ago." The Middle Ages are discussed instead as characterized by "a relative void with respect to scientific thinking and humane treatment of the mentally disturbed." The mass madness and abnormal behavior that characterized the Middle Ages has been attributed to the collapse of medieval institutions and the climate of unrest resulting from wars, revolts, uprisings and plagues. Comparisons might be made between the social climate of the Middle Ages and the social climate of today.

Sandi Gallant's charge that human beings are "animals" is extreme and the claim that "children don't make up these stories" doesn't address the fact that most of the stories in question are being told by middle-aged adults, ususally after long-term therapy or involvement in survivors groups (Principle 4—when in doubt, abort further interaction by playing "Ain't it Awful").

The well-founded skepticism that the promoters of survivor psychology find so deplorable is not limited to the issues of child sexual abuse, satanic cult abuse and the process of recovery or pseudo-psychoanalysis that implants or constructs repressed memories of such abuse. The scientific process of proposing a hypothesis from observation, testing the hypothesis through research, study and experimentation, and reporting results that will be evaluated by other researchers is the scientific and academic method. The research methodology, the population sample and other elements that determine credibility will always be scrutinized. A good theory or hypothesis is one that can be explained, tested and revised. The sexual abuse, incest, satanic abuse and repressed trauma memories theories are far too important in terms of personal, scientific and social impact to go untested and unchallenged. If the promoters of these theories refuse to support their claims, and refuse to refer claims of murder and infanticide for investigation to the proper authorities, the alleged victims refuse to provide evidence and therapists refuse to provide data that proves their therapeutic modalities are helpful, then concerned citizens, law enforcement officials, academics, mental health professionals, researchers and social scientists must get involved.

The history of mental health practices and theories has a long tradition of quackery, magical thinking, mysticism, puritanism, moralism, perfectionism, irrational belief, coercion, superstition and highly profitable, but factually and scientifically unsupportable theories that become fads. The growing skepticism about the recovery culture and the survivor psychology movement is consistent with the critical movement that has evolved in tandem with the American obsession with therapy, psychoanalysis, psychiatry and self-improvement. However, this time the criticisms are not merely good-natured and entertaining accounts of the amusing but harmless human propensity for gullibility. No one engaged in lawsuits or custody battles because they believed Norman Vincent Peale when he told them to "think happy thoughts." But battle lines are being drawn everywhere because people believe a survivor psychologist such as Renee Fredrickson when she says that clients will become healthy, happy, prosperous and productive individuals if they will just "write the unthinkable and say the unspeakable" with the tools they are learning to use in therapy, groups and through survivor manifestoes.

Chapter Seven

Body Memories and Other Pseudoscientific Notions of Survivor Psychology

Show me a sane man and I will cure him for you.

—Carl G. Jung

One of the most commonly used theories to support the ideology of repressed memories or incest and sexual abuse amnesia is "body memories." Many lesser known, but equally unscientific and bogus theories are used in the neo-psychological system of sexual abuse syndromes as well. After presenting a brief history of the supporting rationales commonly used and how the notion of body memories has been used in various questionable, exploitative and quack health and mind-cure systems, the six most common forms of the "body memory" misconceptions will be outlined. The complete transcripts of questions pertaining to these notions from my 1992 survey are presented, with the misconceptions in bold type. The name and number of the misconception and a brief explanation appear in the parentheses within the transcripts. In some cases the model of persuasion, the survivor logic principle, the therapeutic ideology or category of misconception appear in parentheses, with some editorializing within the transcripts.

The Body Remembers What the Mind Forgets?

Body memories are thought to literally be emotional, kinesthetic or chemical recordings stored at the cellular level and retrievable by returning to or recreating the chemical, emotional or kinesthetic conditions under which the memory recordings were filed. This is a bogus application of the notion of "state dependent learning."

The term body memories is used to describe feelings for

which the individual usually has no visual, auditory or other sensory memory imprint. It is claimed that the cells, DNA or simply the body contain 100 percent recall of what the mind represses or forgets. The notion of body memories is based on the idea that the body has no intellectual defenses and cannot "screen out" memory imprints, and the corresponding erroneous idea that even though the mind "records" everything that happens, many memories will remain unavailable because of the power of the mind.

The theory of body memories is not consistent with somatopsychic disorders in which the origin of a psychiatric disorder is physical. The concept of body memories presupposes that the body is capable of harboring or retaining memories, and operates by an independent intelligence which attempts to communicate to the individual about the repressed abuse by literally manifesting signs, diseases or stigmata.

Numerous medical diseases are attributed to repressed abuse such as cancer of the uterus, vagina or breasts, various gynecological problems, and other diseases and afflictions. According to survivor psychologists, the addictive disorders can all be direct results of repressed abuse.

The Misapplication of the "State Dependent Learning Theory" and the "Traumatic Memory Theory"

The body memory notion is bolstered up by two major survivor psychology theories which have been adapted from traditional theories to weave a superficially plausible and official-sounding supporting argument. These two notions are the traumatic memory theory and the state dependent learning or memory theory. According to survivor psychologists, it is possible to retrieve memories of early infancy and even of being in the womb. These "memories" are identified by the survivor psychology version of "state dependency," which means that regression to developmental stages for which no cognitive structure exists will produce "memories" in the manner in which they were imprinted. For instance, survivors subscribing to this theory have reported feeling teething pain, losing the ability to read, losing motor control, loss of speech and blurry vision, all characteristic of infancy. If a client reports somatic sensations such as feeling suffocated or in terror while in a regressed state, these feelings or sensations are considered "proof" of infantile sexual abuse.

Developmental stages of comprehension and cognitive abilities present at the time in which abuse allegedly occurred supposedly "fixes" the memory or knowing at that stage of comprehension. These stages are supposedly consistent with "symptoms" of abuse that manifest in adults in the process of traumatic memory construction. The age at which sexual abuse allegedly occurred is pin-pointed by physical "symptoms" or somatic sensations that supposedly correspond to developmental stages. For instance, if an adult becomes tongue-tied during a regression, trance or "abreaction," they are presumed to be on the infant level because an infant has very little control of the tongue. When a client in hypnosis or regression experiences feelings of terror, rage or being restrained, but cannot articulate the sources of these feelings, it is assumed that they are recovering "memories" of infantile sexual abuse. One "survivor" reported experiencing blurry vision and losing the ability to read. This was interpreted as proof that she was in the infant state, and the feelings she experienced in trance were the state dependent or "developmentally appropriate" means of remembering. Therefore, her feelings of rage and suffocation were interpreted as molestation in early infancy by her father.

The survivor psychology version of the traumatic memory concept is very loosely based on Freud's therapy of repression and Piaget's theory of cognitive development in children, which says that children function primarily through the senses until the age of six or seven. Abstract thinking processes do not normally begin until the age of about seven or eight. Therefore, traumatic memories, extending as far back as the womb, but usually the first six months of life, are supposedly imprinted as sensory memories which may have no cognitive support. The theory was explained by one survivor in the following way: ". . . it's not like I remember picking up a Cheerio this morning, and it got stuck in my throat. That's a memory. What a traumatic memory is—I remember the feeling of the Cheerio being stuck in my throat. Traumatic memories come with the developmental age at which they happened."

Traumatic memories are thought to be "stored" differently than other memories. It is believed by survivor psychologists that they are sealed away, compartmentalized or encapsulated and preserved in pure form, waiting for a "safe" time to be accessed or "triggered," either spontaneously (supposedly when the person is ready), or through therapy, when they have "guidance."

The phrases developmentally appropriate or developmentally inappropriate are also used to reframe past behavior or events that the client did not originally identify as abusive. Developmentally appropriate stages, responses or reactions are said to occur in a fairly consistent manner, and a child acting above or below a developmental stage is being, or has been, abused somehow.

Regression and reliving "repressed" trauma is essential to the theory of how healing occurs in survivor psychology. In survivor psychology theory, the client must return to the "ego" state, or developmental stage, in which abuse occurred in order to "heal" the wound from that stage and grow up.

The History of the Body Memory Notion
The notion of body memories has been recycled many

164

times as a foundational or supportive theory in many quack counseling systems, eccentric philosophical systems and pseudoscientific or metaphysical health and healing cults. The theory of body memories is a fascinating example of a seemingly logical theory that is not only mistaken, it is dangerously coercive.

Survivor psychologists frequently claim that body memories take the form of stigmata, manifesting actual physical representations of events, such as "handprints appearing around a survivor's neck" or acute attacks of pain in the area that was purportedly abused.

Possibly the first time the "cellular memory" or body memory notion surfaced as a persuasion and constructed evidence tactic in survivor literature was in *Michelle Remembers*, the 1980 book that greatly contributed to the satanic abuse legends circulating in the therapeutic community. Michelle had a recurring rash on her forearms and an asymmetrical rash on her neck that was labeled a body memory of Satan's tail, which had supposedly been wrapped around Michelle's neck during a demonic rape. According to Dr. Lawrence Pazder, the devil had literally manifested at a satanic ceremony and wrapped his fiery tail around Michelle's neck and burned the imprint into her flesh.

The idea that emotional reactions and symptoms of stress that manifest in flushing, tremors, shaking, changes in skin color or evenness, or that hives and spots that appear on client's faces, necks arms or legs, are literal "storyboards" or histories written on the body to be "read" by therapists is a very unfortunate development that has fully constellated in survivor psychology. These notions are related to "molecular memory" or cellular memory theories that resurface frequently in quasi-scientific and quasi-paranormal literature. Occasionally a credentialed scientist becomes intrigued with cellular memory theories and begins doing research. This was the case with a recent revival of the molecular memory theory, called one of the ten greatest hoaxes of the 1980s by Bill Lawren in *Omni* magazine.

The survivor psychology explanations of how the mind or body "stores" memories bears a striking similarity to the molecular memory theory proposed in the mid-1980s by Dr. Jacques Benveniste, an immunologist at French National Institute of Health and Medical Research. Benveniste describes molecular memory as ". . . a subtle electromagnetic language that enables one molecule to record the 'essence' of a second, much like a tape recorder records a sound." According to Benveniste, his work could vindicate the discredited field of homeopathy and lead to "the medicine of the future." Benveniste believed that doctors could learn to tap into the "electromagnetic molecular communication system" and, in effect, perform psychic surgery by learning the language of the molecules and giving them signals in that language. Aspirin or other medications could be administered metaphorically, by telling the molecules the biochemical "signal" that translates as aspirin or other medication in molecular language.

Benveniste performed a series of experiments that he claimed proved his hypotheses and submitted a report to *Nature* in 1986. His results were published in 1988, which brought on scrutiny and criticism from the scientific community. A team of investigators, including one with a reputation as a "scientific sheriff" and noted skeptic James Randi, began analyzing Benveniste's research methodology and trying to replicate the results he reported using his methods. All of the tests were negative, but after the initial controversy died down Benveniste began repeating his original trials and is still claiming positive results.

The electromagnetic or biochemical "energy frequency" of certain emotional events that are "stored" or "remembered" by their frequency is the physiological explanation of body memories. Like Benveniste's molecular memory theory, the "traumatic memories" supposedly stored in the cells have their own "language" or means by which they are accessed. Therefore, the therapist must take the client back to the emotional state and developmental stage at which the memories were "recorded" and activate the biochemical or electromagnetic frequency at which the memories are "stored." While abreacting, or literally in the age regressed states at which trauma supposedly occurred, the cells will "release" the memories or reproduce the physiological, emotional and cognitive states and "replicate" the experience for the client. The client has then "disempowered" the memory, and can now metaphorically go back and change the outcome or accept their past powerlessness and grieve it. None of these memory storage or retrieval theories are supported by any scientific data.

Physiological psychologist Karl Lashley used the term "engram," meaning memory trace, in his 25-year search for precise storage sites of memory traces in the brains of rats. Lashley taught rats to run mazes, and systematically removed sections of their cortexes. Lashley was repeatedly disappointed as the rats became increasingly impaired according to how much brain tissue they lost, but they were still able to navigate the mazes. By 1956 Lashley was forced to conclude that memory traces, or engrams, did not have localized sites of storage but were diffused throughout the brain.

By 1948, L. Ron Hubbard had adopted Lashley's theory of engrams, but ignored the results of 25 years of research. Hubbard decided that all neuroses, psychoses and illnesses were caused by cellular recordings or imprints. He claimed that he wrote the self-described "completely scientific report," *Dianetics*, in three weeks. According to Martin Gardner, author of *Fads and Fallacies in the Name of Science*, this is not hard to believe because nothing in the book resembles a scientific report, and the "case studies" were constructed from Hubbard's memory and imagination.

Dianetics is a Greek word meaning "thought." Hubbard's philosophy was that words are imprinted in the cells of the body, particularly in the developing fetus, and even in a sperm or an egg, prior to conception. According to Hubbard's theories, the subconscious mind, or "reactive mind," is completely literal, and all uncomfortable sensations, painful experiences or words heard in the womb and in early childhood are imprinted in the cells and literally interpreted and manifested as neuroses, psychosomatic disorders and diseases by the body throughout life unless they are "audited out." Auditing is merely a process of hypnosis, which is called a "dianetic reverie." The client is regressed and aggressively questioned and coerced to make connections between current problems and diseases to early memories or pre-birth traumas. Dianetic belief systems and procedures bear striking similarities to body memory notions and the memory retrieval practices of therapists subscribing to survivor psychology theories.

When the therapist interprets flushing, hives, rashes, headaches, stomachaches and other physiological sensations of stress and emotional arousal as signs or forms of "memory" during counseling sessions, hypnosis or group therapy, the notion of body memories becomes a means of indoctrination in survivor logic. When therapists teach clients that everything from the common cold to cancer are forms of body memories, clients develop attentional biases or predispositions to interpret everything from mundane sensations to serious illnesses as body memories. This pseudoscientific means of divination used by therapists to convince clients with no memories of sexual abuse that they are "survivors" is not responsible, credible or supportable.

There are many physiological diseases, symptoms and

sensations that are confusing and frightening. The "mind-cure, spirit-cure" philosophies that claim people cause or choose their own diseases, and are entirely responsible for "creating their own realities," leave many people with a sense of guilt, distress, shame and a desperate need to explain the unknown. The cause-and-effect body memory theory provides a logical explanation for the common problems women experience, particularly since some of the most frequently mentioned "symptoms" of repressed incest and sexual abuse are said to be vaginal pain, yeast infections, or any problem with female reproductive organs. The seduction of the "explanation delusion" or "the logical fallacy of the false cause" exploits the powerful human need to know, explain and make sense out of chaotic or mysterious events and phenomena.

Six Categories of Misconceptions About Body Memories

According to the survivor manifestoes and the answers given by the therapists in my survey, there are six common categories of misconceptions regarding body memories. Survivor psychologists tend to explain body memories as: 1) a "sensory memory" or somatic storage mode in which physical symptoms of repressed memories manifest in variety of ways from cancer to pimples; 2) a biological explanation of memory; 3) the memory stigmata theory; 4) a variation of the slogan popularized by *The Courage to Heal* — "The body remembers what the mind forgets;" 5) the logical fallacy of the false cause; and 6) mumbo jumbo.

Category #1: Somatic Complaints/Sensory Memory Storage Theory—Diseases, various types of pain and other somatic sensations are reframed as "body memories."

Category #2: Cellular/Biological Memory Storage Theory—The therapists and counselors talk vaguely about "cellular memory storage," yet few were able to offer any explanation for how the cells "stored" memories. The study subjects who attempted to explain cellular memory storage offered sadly deluded and scientifically illiterate explanations.

Category #3: Memory Stigmata Theory— Various mundane physiological reactions are literally interpreted by the therapist as actual representations of events that had occurred in the past. Physiological or emotional reactions during regressions, trances, abreactions and formal hypnosis are considered "proof" of repressed abuse.

Category #4: *The Courage to Heal* **Slogan**—The body memory theories are variations of the slogan "The body remembers what the mind forgets."

Category #5: The Logical Fallacy of the False Cause Theory—Creating an explanation for a physiological/emotional/psychological syndrome or a mysterious or mundane event, after the fact. Making sense out of that which had no explanation and usually needed none before traumatic reframing and survivor logic indoctrination. From the transcripts it is obvious that these therapists are reframing medical diagnoses in emotional terms, and apparently taking a lengthy, but superficial medical history from clients. In some cases therapists appear to be acting outside of the range of their profession and even diverting clients away from medical doctors and medical help. This is not only unethical, it may be dangerous.

Category #6: Mumbo Jumbo, or completely meaningless or indecipherable explanations.

The complete transcripts of questions 10, 11, 12 and 12A of the structured interview survey follow this section and the misconceptions are highlighted in bold type and numbered to show how prevalent these six categories of misconceptions are and to show how they are used as persuasion tactics on clients using the three models of persuasion. Various coercive therapeutic modalities and ideologies have already been explained. The modalities and ideologies are also named, so expect to see "state dependent learning theory," "attentional bias," "selective reinforcement" of so-called symptoms, and so on, in parentheses along side the therapist's answers as well. The approximate percentages of clients each therapist claims experience body memories is also highlighted in bold type. The questions pertaining to body memories are listed below.

Question #10: *Could you describe the concept of body memories?*
Question #11: *Could you explain how the body stores memories?*
Question #12: *Approximately what percentage of your clients experience body memories?*
Question #12A: *How can you tell when a client is experiencing a body memory?*

In some cases, issues related to the above questions are pursued in more detail as the course of the interview lent itself to further exploration. As a result, other questions may appear that are consistent with the subject matter.

Partial Results of the Structured Interview Survey Regarding "Body Memories"

Overall, the therapists in the survey claimed that 59 percent of their clients experienced body memories. Ninety-five percent of the therapists said it was common for memories to surface via body memories. Several therapists claimed 100 percent of their clients experienced body memories if they were "working it through" (in reference to traumatic memories), or if they were sexual abuse survivors. This is where the beliefs and biases got really interesting. Therapists often reported that their regular client load, or those without sexual abuse issues, did not generally experience body memories, that this "symptom" of repressed traumatic memories was usually unique only to traumatic memories of sexual abuse.

Why body memories would be specific to traumatic memories of sexual abuse is a curious assumption. It would seem that if the body had the capability to "record" traumatic experiences, it would record all traumatic experiences. It is also curious that body memories would specifically deal with infantile sexual abuse. If the cognitive processes are not developed enough to recognize, understand or remember sexual abuse, how would the body know the difference between sexual trauma and any trauma? Trauma would simply be recorded as trauma, if the theory had any validity at all. The fact that many therapists believed that body memories of preverbal trauma were only of a sexual nature demonstrated clearly illogical biases and ideologies.

Complete Transcript of Questions #10, #11, #12 and #12A of the Structured Interview Survey with Sexual Abuse Counselors

Subject #1:
Could you describe the concept of body memories?
"Yes. What I see is that even though . . . Let me share with you a person. When I first started working with someone and they were talking about their father and they dissociated in the middle of that and they were like reacting, like he was in the room right then and not only did their whole body shake, especially **like you could see like the goose bumps and the redness all up and down their legs, but you could also see like a hand print across her throat. It's like even though she didn't really remember it consciously what was happening, her body registered what happened. And when she moved into that place**

again, you could physically see what happened (#3—
memory stigmata theory; traumatic reframing; attentional
bias). That's like, like an extreme case but different people
have different levels of that."

*Does the concept of body memories correspond to the concept
of cellular memories?*

"Do you know, I'm not really sure how other people
explain it? I don't know that I'm the best expert on that. I
mean, in my own mind **I have related it to state dependent
learning, the way that we store things, that our brains
biochemically store things based on the chemistry of
what's going on in their body at the time** (#2—bogus
biological, biochemical theory to support the ideology of
body memories). And so, when it's repressed, our whole
body will respond."

*Could you describe that process somewhat? Like what is a
cellular memory?*

"Once again, I'm probably, as far as what's written in the
literature, I don't know that I can. I just know what I see
therapeutically."

That's all I'm asking for.

"Which is that somebody's, **it's like even when they
don't have conscious memory of it, it still registers in
their cells, in their feelings** (#2—cellular/biological theory;
traumatic reframing). **Sometimes like in teaching a class
if I'm talking about different things, and even if someone
doesn't connect with them personally, they'll get stomach
aches, or cramps, or their throat will hurt. They'll get
physical, like cellular reactions to what's being said. I
believe that's a form of remembering**" (#1—sensory
memory theory; attentional bias; traumatic reframing).

*Approximately what percentage of your clients experience
body memories?*

"**Actually, they are probably the same number, at least
half. Most people, if they know and they're willing to**

work on that, then they always feel safe with me and they will go into those places" (hypnotic model of persuasion; "safe" theory).

How can you tell when a client is experiencing a body memory?

"They are no longer connected in the here and now. They're usually, you know, usually, **once I'm safe with someone and they dissociate when we're talking about something, I will go with them to where they go and in that process, I'll start to notice all the physical symptoms start happening, because there's almost always body memories there**" (inadvertent hypnosis; attentional bias; selective reinforcement).

Subject #2:

Could you describe the concept of body memories?

"Let's see, **what I believe is that memories can be stored in the tissues of the body. And sometimes people will begin to have symptomatology around their bodies before they have cognitive memories** (#2—cellular memory storage theory; traumatic reframing). Some examples of that are **sometimes people have a sense of their being restrained or tied up or something like that and they will have a distinct sensation of that around their wrists. Sometimes people have vaginal pain** (#1—sensory memory). So my understanding of body memories, that is what it is."

Do you have any more technical terminology to describe how memories are stored in the tissues of the body?

"(Laughs) **Well I guess I just believe that sometimes the body remembers when the mind can't**" (#4—*The Courage to Heal* slogan).

Does the concept of body memories correspond to the concept of cellular memories?

"Yes."

Approximately what percentage of your clients experience body memories?

"Of the 80 to 90 percent of the clients I see that have sexual abuse history, probably less than half of those have body memories, maybe even less than that, but you know sometimes they have a lot of somatic complaints that might really be about their histories, but in terms of identifying it, them identifying it as a body memory, or even me, identifying it as body memory, it would probably be in the neighborhood of about 30 to 40 percent."

How can you tell when a client is experiencing a body memory?

"Well, I can't and they can't always tell that. Sometimes it's absolutely unmistakable. But in most cases that's not so. In most cases there's other ways to explain it . . . you know more logical, rational present day things to explain it. **The kinds of clients that I find that have body memories where it's clearest, to me and to them, are my clients who have ritual history**" (attentional bias).

Subject #3:

Could you describe the concept of body memories?

"You want me to define it?"

Yes.

"Okay, **how I would define body memories are when there's twitching or sensation, oh, such as something hot or cold or you can feel something pressing onto your body but you can't see anything. And, you don't have an actual memory in the intellectual realm**" (#1 and #6—a totally meaningless sensory memory theory; traumatic reframing; attentional bias).

Does the concept of body memories correspond to the concept of cellular memories?

"It does with me."

Could you describe cellular memories?

"Okay, to me **cellular memories are similar to what I just described and oftentimes there are actual data that comes up with it at the same time that people have often** reported as thinking that maybe it didn't happen in this lifetime, that it happened in some other lifetime (#5— logical fallacy of the false cause). Or, that it did happen in this lifetime but they don't have memory of it happening to them, so it has the sensation along with memory, frequently."

Okay, how would you access that then?

"You mean how do I get the client into that place?"

Yes, or how was the information accessed?

"Well, in a variety of ways. Sometimes it's spontaneous where this stuff is happening to them and they don't know what it is, and so, I'll say, 'well, this looks like a body memory.' So, sometimes I tell them. Since it's going on and they don't know what it is, so I say this is what a body memory looks like. I define it and describe it** (therapeutic language; traumatic reframing; the learning model of persuasion). They are the ones that then validate if that's what it is or not. Another way is through imagery, eyes closed, or visualization work, where they go into, they journey into the imagination or consciousness, whatever you want to call it, with their eyes closed and recall a memory. And in the recall of that memory frequently they will go into what I would call a regression. Which is they leave this time and space and enter into that memory time and space"** (hypnotic model of persuasion; traumatic remembering).

Approximately what percentage of your clients experience body memories?

"I would say 95 percent."

How can you tell when a client is experiencing a body memory?

"Well, I don't think it's yes or no. What I have to do is tell them what I'm observing, check it out with them** (traumatic reframing; selective reinforcement). They have to give me feedback and we have to work back and forth with this. I don't think that as a responsible counselor, I can say absolutely that that's what's happening to them. It has to be a partnership."

Subject #4:

Could you describe the concept of body memories?

"Where the conscious mind doesn't remember the traumatic event from the past, usually childhood, but it is in fact stored in the body (#2—cellular memory storage). And **something in the current life will trigger the body to feel like intense fear or intense anger, though the mind at the moment doesn't have a clue of what that intense body connection or what that body reaction is connected to"** (#2—sensory memory "trigger" theory; traumatic reframing; the learning model of persuasion).

Does the concept of body memories correspond to the concept of cellular memories?

"Yes."

Is there some way you could describe that, like how does the body store memories?

"I don't think anybody really knows that, as yet."

But the concept of cellular memories and body memories are similar concepts?

"They are to me."

Approximately what percentage of your clients experience body memories?

"Gosh, I don't know. **I'll guess 33 percent."**

How can you tell when a client is experiencing a body memory?

"Well, they'll describe it to me."

Well, can you describe that a little bit more, like what would be happening?

"Oh, okay. They might be shaking very heavily, as in a major fear reaction to something that they, that triggered them in their present life, like looking at a certain picture or driving by a certain house."

Subject #5:
Could you describe the concept of body memories?

"Body memories are those things that may happen within the body physically that may be, if ruled out as having no medical basis, may be recurring; however, there are many body memories that are also medically based and I would suggest that they work with a doctor who is aware of those, a medical doctor who is aware of that" (#1—somatic complaints; sensory memory storage theory).

Does the concept of body memories correspond to the concept of cellular memories?

"Yes. **Well I think that whatever happens to us the body remembers in great detail and doesn't lose it"** (#4—variation of Bass and Davis slogan).

Could you describe how the body stores memories or how memories are stored on a cellular level?

"No, I probably couldn't. I'm not educated in that part as far as, I believe in the concept. Let's put it that way. I don't know how it does it and I don't know that anybody at this point knows how it does it."

Approximately what percentage of your clients experience body memories?

"Of the sexual clients? I'd say I don't know of any that haven't, oh, 95 percent" (attentional bias).

How can you tell when a client is experiencing a body memory?
"No, generally the client will tell me."

Subject #6:
Could you describe the concept of body memories?

"Even though the abuse for some is conscious and the abuse for some is unconscious, the trauma is held, I believe, in the cellular level (#2—cellular/biological theory). So often a person will be, again, sometimes it's conscious, sometimes it's unconscious. **I've had it where bruises reappear where, I had one woman that was burned with ciga-**

rettes, the welts reappear (#3—memory stigmata theory). Sometimes is not in the physical but more of the, you know, **'I just feel like there are hands on my body'** (#1—somatic sensations). That sort of stuff. And **I always explain it as that's the healing process. That's the body releasing it and it's moving out, even though it's terrifying, that's a positive. So, I try to help them understand what's going on and make sense of that reality"** (therapeutic thinking; survivor logic; the learning model of persuasion).

Does the concept of body memories correspond to the concept of cellular memories?

"I think so."

Approximately what percentage of your clients experience body memories?

"Say 40 percent."

How can you tell when a client is experiencing a body memory?

"Usually they'll report it. I mean if they're just sitting there, I can't say I think somebody's choking you now. Usually, they will, I can tell because they're giving me, I mean I can tell if they're getting terrified and I say, 'What's happening? What's going on with you now?' but it's usually because of what they're giving me."

Subject #7:

Could you describe the concept of body memories?

"Physical sensations" (#1— somatic complaints or sensations).

Does the concept of body memories correspond to the concept of cellular memories?

"I don't know."

Approximately what percentage of your clients experience body memories?

"Fifty percent."

How can you tell when a client is experiencing a body memory?

"I can't always."

Subject #8:
Could you describe the concept of body memories?

"My description would be **feelings or pain in the body that doesn't seem to have any connection with what's happening at the moment**" (#1—somatic complaints; sensory impressions; #5—logical fallacy of the false cause; survivor logic; propaganda model of persuasion).

Does the concept of body memories correspond to the concept of cellular memories?

"I never thought about that, Susan, but probably so."

Do you understand the concept of cellular memories? What is the concept?

"In my thinking **it's like the Reichian theory that we hold our emotions and or memories in our body, in cells of our body, literally, and that our cells have memories. That the memories are not just in the brain, they're in our bodies**" (#2—cellular/biological theory).

Approximately what percentage of your clients experience body memories?

"**Probably 20 percent. Wait, that's probably not true. It's probably more than 30 percent.**"

Can you tell when a client is experiencing a body memory?

"Sometimes."

Subject #9:
Could you describe the concept of body memories?

"Okay, body memories. It's a **cellular memory of trauma that often is not related to any cognitive memory of the event**" (#2—cellular/biological theory).

Does the concept of body memories correspond to the concept of cellular memories?

"Yes."

Approximately what percentage of your clients experience body memories?

"**That talks about it, I would say 20 percent.**"

Can you tell when a client is experiencing a body memory?
"No, but they can."

Subject #10:
Could you describe the concept of body memories?
"Yes, I've had **people who present themselves as having like phantom pain. They're not real. Maybe having pain periodically in the anus and having that checked out for physical causes and there's no physical, actual reason that you don't have problems like with stools that would create that, but they would have that pain and there's no reasonable explanation for it"** (#1—somatic complaints; sensory impressions; survivor logic; propaganda model of persuasion).

Does the concept of body memories correspond to the concept of cellular memories?
"Well, no I don't see it as quite the same thing."

Could you describe the concept or the theory of cellular memories?
"No, but **body memories to me are when a child is abused, or a person is abused, that information is being input and recorded in the entire system, so even if the mind doesn't remember it, your body has learned through the neuro-pathways and the biochemical changes that result when people are having the experience, that something is happening to them** (#2—biological theory). They have an emotional response and through their emotions have biochemical changes you may create as well."

Approximately what percentage of your clients experience body memories?
"I've had a smaller percentage of people who do that. **People who have no recollection of having been sexually abused seem to have more in the way of body memories** (selective reinforcement; attentional bias). So, **I would guess that maybe of those who have repressed, maybe 15 per-**

cent of those have body memories. It helps them to further access some of the information."

How can you tell when a client is experiencing a body memory?

"Well, part of that is self-report and sometimes by just watching them. How they carry themselves, what they do. You know I may ask them, 'What's going on right now?' and somebody will say, 'Well, I just had this feeling, like a real sensitive area on my thigh, and there's no reason for that but I know I've had that feeling before and it doesn't seem to connect with anything'" (#5—logical fallacy; traumatic reframing).

Subject #11:

Could you describe the concept of body memories?

"Body memories are feelings in the body that were probably taken in by the child when the child was very young and so the child may be pre-verbal and can't remember or get it into a logical sequence and be able to talk about it very well, but they have the felt sensations. So, I'd say body memories are these felt sensations of what happened to them" (#1—sensory memory theory).

Does the concept of body memories correspond to the concept of cellular memories?

"Yes, I do believe that, yes."

Approximately what percentage of your clients experience body memories?

"Many, I think all of them to some degree and it all depends on the age and the type of abuse."

How can you tell when a client is experiencing a body memory?

"I find that there is actual body twitching, body movement and sometimes a client complains of feelings of warmth or wetness, or that kind of thing" (#6—mumbo jumbo—from symptoms this vague all you could reasonably conclude is that the client is alive).

Subject #12:
Could you describe the concept of body memories?
"No."
Does the concept of body memories correspond to the concept of cellular memories?
"I don't have anything on that."
Approximately what percentage of your clients experience body memories?
"I don't feel like I know enough of an accurate definition of that to answer accurately."
How can you tell when a client is experiencing a body memory?
"I don't know."

Subject #13:
Could you describe the concept of body memories?
"A body memory is either a pain or some physical reproducing of a bruise or a welt that occurs" (#3—memory stigmata theory).
Does the concept of body memories correspond to the concept of cellular memories?
"Yes. Well, you can't have a body memory unless the cells are operating in such a way (#6—mumbo jumbo). To me they are one in the same. Both are operating at the same time. **I believe the body never forgets an experience and that would be contained in the cells of the body** (#4— variation of Bass and Davis slogan; survivor logic; propaganda model of persuasion). I don't make a big distinction like some people do."
Approximately what percentage of your clients experience body memories?
"I think 100 percent experience body memories if you're doing deep feelings work with them. Eventually they're going to experience it" (attentional bias; selective reinforcement).
How can you tell when a client is experiencing a body memory?

"I check out by questioning what the various parts of their body is feeling and I look for different responses and effectual responses that may cue me they're having one."

Subject #14:
No data for questions 10 and 11 (tape malfunction).
Approximately what percentage of your clients experience body memories?
"All."
How can you tell when a client is experiencing a body memory?
"They signal when hypnotically regressed (hypnotic model of persuasion)."

Subject #15:
Could you describe the concept of body memories?
"If a person is having memories or flashes or blips of abuse that occurred they usually will have some kind of somatic response from part of the body. That somatic response may be anything from welts or pimples to severe cramping to major pain" (#1—somatic theory; traumatic reframing).
Does the concept of body memories correspond to the concept of cellular memories?
"I don't know."
Approximately what percentage of your clients experience body memories?
"Probably all of them."
How can you tell when a client is experiencing a body memory?
"They usually double up in my office."

Subject #16:
Could you describe the concept of body memories?
"Okay, the way I see it is that people may not have a visual memory in their mind, or a cognitive memory of abuse but they may with a trigger, for instance, a dream

or just hearing about something, they may experience pain or discomfort in their body. And that may or may not be in a sexual feeling. It may be a pain in their neck that is recurring (#5—logical fallacy of the false cause). So in other words, when someone's getting close to remembering something, they may have the beginning of the memory in their body (traumatic reframing). Or, for instance, I've had people in their wrists, aching in their wrists have, you know, because that's come about later that they were held by their wrists, or during the abuse" (#1—sensory memory theory; traumatic reframing; survivor logic; propaganda model of persuasion).

Does the concept of body memories correspond to the concept of cellular memories?

"For me it does."

Could you describe cellular memories in a little more detail and more technically?

"I don't know if I can do it technically, but the way I conceptualize that is that I feel that all the memory, the memory of traumatic events is stored cellularly (#2—cellular memory storage theory). And so that when the memory begins to become known, that the repression is reversed, for instance, the cells actually recall the experience and there could be, there almost could be like a flooding of toxicity in the body, so there could be a lot of anxiety due to adrenaline. Or sickness, like flu-like symptoms, for instance, you know, nausea, vomiting, diarrhea, and so, I believe that's essentially the trauma. It then can be stored at a cellular level" (#2 and #6—official sounding cellular memory mumbo jumbo; survivor logic; propaganda model of persuasion).

Approximately what percentage of your clients experience body memories?

"Of the sexual abuse people, I'd say 70 to 80 percent" (selective attention).

How can you tell when a client is experiencing a body memory?

"Well, it's obvious in their body. I guess you, I look for any signs that, if they continue to rub their necks, for instance, or shift around a lot, I would just look for non-verbal clues that something's happening to them physically and then ask them, you know, what they're experiencing in their body, or have they been having persistent symptoms when they leave therapy, or for the next few days, that type of thing" (attentional bias; traumatic reframing).

Subject #17:

Could you describe the concept of body memories?

"Body memories are physical symptoms that cannot be explained or diagnosed" (#6—completely meaningless statement).

Does the concept of body memories correspond to the concept of cellular memories? Have you heard those two used interchangeably?

"No, I don't use them interchangeably."

Is there any relationship with the two ideas?

"Yes, I guess there could be some relationship."

Okay, could you explain cellular memories a little more?

"Cellular memories in my understanding are that the very, within each cell there's a mitochondria that has the capacity for recording events" (#2 and #6—bogus biological theory).

Approximately what percentage of your clients experience body memories?

"Maybe 50 percent."

How can you tell when a client is experiencing a body memory?

"Well, they will talk about having a pain and they can associate the pain in their body with some thoughts about abuse" (traumatic reframing).

Subject #18:
Could you describe the concept of body memories?

"Well, I think that is any kinesthetic experience by someone that is regressive in nature and doesn't have to do with something that's going on in their lives here and now" (#1, #5 and #6—sensory or somatic impression theory that makes no sense but offers an official sounding explanation).

Does the concept of body memories correspond to the concept of cellular memories?

"I don't know about cellular memories."

Approximately what percentage of your clients experience body memories?

"Twenty-five percent, maybe."

How can you tell when a client is experiencing a body memory?

"Well, usually they are describing some kind of kinesthetic experience that doesn't have anything to do with what's going on in their lives right now and that's distressing to them. That's why they are bringing it up. Usually when we track it in trance, it goes back to a specific sexual abuse memory or cult memory" (traumatic reframing; survivor logic).

Subject #19:
Could you describe the concept of body memories?

"Body memories are similar to having a flashback or remembering something, but it's more like your body's experiencing it" (#1—sensory impression theory).

Does the concept of body memories correspond to the concept of cellular memories?

"I'm not too sure what cellular memories are."

Approximately what percentage of your clients experience body memories?

"Maybe 30 percent."

How can you tell when a client is experiencing a body memory?

"They dissociate, meaning they get a blank stare, something like that. They may feel just a lot of terror all through their bodies. I just had a girl yesterday become totally frightened and scared and she couldn't move any part of her body. That kind of thing, or another woman I worked with felt like there was fur in her mouth and she couldn't get it out. That kind of thing" (# 5—logical fallacy).

Subject #20:
Could you describe the concept of body memories?

"It's when you don't have a cognitive or a mental image but your body remembers a traumatic event or something that's happened to it, so the memory is in your body. Like, for instance, somebody that was forced to have oral sex with her father might have a gagging response for no reason. You know, her throat is responding to the pressure but there's no pressure there" (#1 and #5— Sensory impression theory; logical fallacy; traumatic reframing).

Does the concept of body memories correspond to the concept of cellular memories?

"I don't know what you mean by cellular."

Approximately what percentage of your clients experience body memories?

"Fifty percent."

How can you tell when a client is experiencing a body memory?

"Just in their non-verbal cues and, you know, their body will either tense up or they'll do something, that'll, you know, be unrelated to what we're talking about" (#5—logical fallacy; attentional bias).

Subject #21:
Could you describe the concept of body memories?

"An unexplained physiological experience, well, basically an unexplained physiological response that is not originating in the moment or the experience going on right now" (#1 and #5—somatic impression theory and logical fallacy; traumatic reframing; the learning model of persuasion).

Does the concept of body memories correspond to the concept of cellular memories?

"No. Wait, do you mean correspond?"

Yes.

"Sometimes."

Approximately what percentage of your clients experience body memories?

"Probably 60 percent."

How can you tell when a client is experiencing a body memory?

"A lot of times self-report."

Subject #22:

Could you describe the concept of body memories?

"Yes. **Body memory would be a memory of some particular type of trauma that is experienced physiologically or physically within the body even though there seems to be no clear explanation of why it is occurring and where it's coming from"** (#1 and #5—somatic impression theory; logical fallacy; traumatic reframing; the learning model of persuasion).

Does the concept of body memories correspond to the concept of cellular memories?

"Cellular memories?"

If you're not familiar with the terminology, you don't have to extrapolate on that. Usually I see those in the literature together implying that cellular memories and body memories are similar concepts. That the cells of the body hold memories.

"Oh, I've heard of that from physical therapists and some massage therapists and so forth, but I haven't, I wouldn't, I haven't explored that end of it enough to really make a comment on that."

Approximately what percentage of your clients experience body memories?

"Sexual abuse clients, probably, eventually I would say probably 90 percent of them" (attentional bias).

How can you tell when a client is experiencing a body memory?

"If they're having one in my office it's pretty clear. If it's not in my office they usually report it to me what, are confused by it, then I describe what a body memory is" (traumatic reframing; learning model of persuasion).

Subject #23:

No data for questions 10 and 11 (tape recorder was not turned on).

Approximately what percentage of your clients experience body memories?

"70 percent."

How can you tell when a client is experiencing a body memory?

"Self-report."

Subject #24:

Could you describe the concept of body memories?

"Yes, what I think is that when people go through traumatic events, what we tend to do is we process that information in any of four different ways. Like cognitively, or emotionally, or physically, you can have your memories divided into different sections (learning model of persuasion). To me, what I think, **what I would recognize as a body memory is a similar sensation that they would have experienced at the time of the event, but they're having it without stimuli in the present"** (#1— sensory memory theory; the learning model of persuasion).

Now you mentioned four processes and you mentioned cognitive and emotional, what other means?

"Yes, I'm forgetting what the fourth one is. I know

there's four but I . . ."

Okay, you've got cognitive, emotional and physical.

"There's a fourth one but I can't think what it is."

Does the concept of body memories correspond to the concept of cellular memories?

"Oh God, I have no idea of even what that means. What does that mean?"

Well, I've read in the literature where they relate those two concepts or use them interchangeably and the theory seems to be that body memories, being stored physically, are stored on the cellular level.

"Oh, it's a physiological explanation for memory?"

Perhaps. I'm not sure that it really is, but that's the way it's used.

Approximately what percentage of your clients experience body memories?

"I think everybody does" (attentional bias).

How can you tell when a client is experiencing a body memory?

"I ask them to describe what's happening to them" (selective reinforcement).

Subject #25:

Could you describe the concept of body memories?

"It's memory that's hidden in their body and usually the mind usually comes before, often comes before the cognitive memory" (#1 and #6—nonsensical sensory theory; survivor logic).

Does the concept of body memories correspond to the concept of cellular memories?

"I suppose so. **I really don't understand but the body seems to carry the physical symptoms often even when the mind doesn't know about them"** (#4—Bass and Davis slogan).

Approximately what percentage of your clients experience body memories?

"Probably 60 percent."

How can you tell when a client is experiencing a body memory?
"They tell me."

Subject #26:
Could you describe the concept of body memories?
"A physical reaction by the body that has been re-pressed just as, uh, from memory by the mind" (#1—sensory memory storage theory).
Does the concept of body memories correspond to the concept of cellular memories?
"Uh, that's a good question. I don't know if I'd put it on the cell level or not."
Approximately what percentage of your clients experience body memories?
"Sixty percent."
How can you tell when a client is experiencing a body memory?
"Their descriptions, their physical presentation of that, both of those. Often most what it is, is a claim. They'll come in and start describing something and say this really weird thing happened or they'll start having an obsession as they're getting a memory" (traumatic reframing).

Subject #27:
Could you describe the concept of body memories?
"No."
Does the concept of body memories correspond to the concept of cellular memories?
"I don't know."
Approximately what percentage of your clients experience body memories?
"Twenty-five to 35 percent."
How can you tell when a client is experiencing a body memory?
"Self-report, shivering, non-verbal changes" (traumatic reframing).

Subject #28:
Could you describe the concept of body memories?

"Yes, it's my understanding that **somebody may or may not have a clear memory of abuse but they'll feel it in their body** (traumatic reframing). And usually the way I find, the way I can tell, well, one of the other things I left out is **if they have body memories be that either pain or it could be sexual in nature and their body's remembering but their mind can't sometimes**" (#4—variation of Bass and Davis slogan).

Does the concept of body memories correspond to the concept of cellular memories?

"Yes, I look at it that way. I mean, **memories are stored and sometimes their consciousness doesn't remember it but their body, which has, you know, neurons and cells, remembers it**" (#2 and #6—embarrassing attempt at a biological theory).

Approximately what percentage of your clients experience body memories?

"**Well, all of them that have been abused, uh, pretty much to one degree or another. Sometimes it's not as strong with some women but it can range from extreme uncomfortableness in being touched, which the body image therapist usually does that stuff to a full-blown feeling like it's happening.**"

How can you tell when a client is experiencing a body memory?

"**They get increasingly anxious. Tense, tight muscles, sometimes they can't move. They may experience pain in a part of their body. Sometimes they get sexual feelings when it's happening, well sometimes they can identify it. Most of them usually get sexual abuse and sexual but they don't identify it as such**" (traumatic thinking).

Subject #29:
Could you describe the concept of body memories?

"The way I understand it, it's that **sometimes trauma is held within the body and might not be conscious in the mind or the emotional body, but the physical body can respond to trauma and be holding the memory**" (# 6 and #2—mumbo jumbo; biological theory).

Does the concept of body memories correspond to the concept of cellular memories?

"For me, yes. Cellular memory I think is that, I think all of our patterns, all of the characterological, defensive patterns that we've developed to deal with are emotional, or physical, or psychological abuse or neglect, those patterns get stored as memory within all of the cells of our being. So cellular memory has to do with maintaining, you know, energetic patterns, whereas body trauma, or body memory might be slightly different in that. I see that as where there's a certain trauma to the physical body, the body actually remembers that and there might be hypersensitivity in that area, or if you stimulate that area the memories might surface."

Approximately what percentage of your clients experience body memories?

"Gosh, maybe 10 to 15 percent."

How can you tell when a client is experiencing a body memory?

"I would say it's real concrete, if a client sometimes is extremely terrified when their partner touches them in a certain area or they relay stories of being touched in a certain way and it evokes memory."

Subject #30:

Could you describe the concept of body memories?

"Sure, that our bodies don't ever forget (#4— *The Courage to Heal* slogan) and that **the body carries sensations that if we pay attention to them can give us feeling labels and thought memories, feelings and thought memories"** (#2 and #6—incomprehensible sensory memory theory in therapeutic language).

Does the concept of body memories correspond to the concept of cellular memories?

"I don't know about cellular memories. Oh, okay, more the Jungian kind of view? It could, yes."

Could you explain how the body stores memories, because that's what the cellular concept generally has to do with. Could you explain further how the body stores memories?

"See, there's a whole new bunch of theories that says there's no such thing as memory. No, I can't."

Approximately what percentage of your clients experience body memories?

"I would say all of the 5 percent that are sexual abuse survivors in my practice."

How can you tell when a client is experiencing a body memory?

"Oh, they move. They either move or there's a motion of some sort" (#6—mumbo jumbo).

Subject #31:

Could you describe the concept of body memories?

"No. I can't put any of that into words this morning."

Does the concept of body memories correspond to the concept of cellular memories?

"I've heard that theory before. I'm not sure that I agree with that."

Approximately what percentage of your clients experience body memories?

"Probably 50 percent."

How can you tell when a client is experiencing a body memory?

"They usually dissociate. They often go into like a fetal position or some sort of a physical protective position. I guess they are like the two things I think of off the top of my head. They act younger. They usually regress" (inadvertent hypnosis).

Subject #32:
Could you describe the concept of body memories?

"Well, I believe that the body in terms of the muscle structures of our body, the skeletal structures of our body does have the ability to have imprinted memory in terms of pain, in terms of being touched and I believe that we are imprinted by touch, and as a result, I believe that there is such a thing as muscle memory, so when certain muscle groups are touched it can trigger the memory process, in terms of subconscious or unconscious recall of repressed material and that in terms of helping clients to recognize when their body is communicating something that often times it will represent something that's happened in the past, that's been cued up by either a touch, by either a smell, by either a familiar event or even a group of words" (#2 and #6—official sounding mumbo jumbo with the sensory memory trigger theory).

Does the concept of body memories correspond to the concept of cellular memories?

"I don't know about that."

Approximately what percentage of your clients experience body memories?

"I would say that's 100 percent."

How can you tell when a client is experiencing a body memory?

"They report usually a common pain that they've had a variety of times in their life that's been unexplained in terms of medical procedures or medical evaluations (#5— traumatic reframing). They will usually put their hand on the area of their body that they're experiencing pain."

When they do that, they're touching themselves, do you interpret that or do they indicate that?

"They, sometimes I'll draw their attention to what they are doing with their hands because it's usually an unconscious process in terms of touching themselves in a particular way and then I will ask them what the touch is about" (selective reinforcement).

Subject #33:
Could you describe the concept of body memories?
"The most frequent time the issue of body memories comes up is when somebody is verging on remembering or they're believing that they're remembering and if they have a particularly eventful session where they get a memory or something happens, then I'll talk to them a little bit about what's normal. That their body might start remembering what happened to them and then give then some partial symptoms some probabilities and usually at the point at which I'm doing that they look very relieved because it's already started (therapeutic thinking; selective attention and reinforcement). And so, they have a sense of 'Yeah, that's happening.' And I tell them, 'You know, I'm not telling you not to go to the doctor, but just be aware that this is very normal and to give it a little bit of time before you decide that something's wrong.' "

Could you describe a little more how the body stores memories or how the body remembers?
"Sometimes I'll talk to them about how cells have memories and that it's very often where the person is traumatized will store memory (#5—logical fallacy). If they were held at the base of the neck, very often they've got neck and shoulder pain. If they were raped orally, very often they've got tension in the jaw area, so I'll talk to them about just very specific things like that but other kinds of body memories like nausea, headaches, those kings of things would again be the body remembering, but that's more a fear response type of remembering or the headaches are more of a blocking, you know, they had to block the memory" (traumatic reframing; selective attention and reinforcement).

Does the concept of body memories correspond to the concept of cellular memories?

"Yes, but **the body remembers just like the mind remembers**" (#4—variation of Bass and Davis slogan).

Approximately what percentage of your clients experience body memories?

"**One hundred percent, if they're working it through**" (attentional bias; response expectancy).

How can you tell when a client is experiencing a body memory?

"**You're asking me to describe intuition. That's one way. Very often they'll tell me. Sometimes I'll have a client on a first session come in and say, 'You know, I don't feel good. I'm nauseous. I have headaches. I don't know what's the matter.' And then, I'll just start questioning them, 'Well, you know, when have you noticed this before? Does it happen to you every year at this time?' Because sometimes a trauma will have happened at a certain time of the year and that time of the year will connect with a memory, kind of like an anniversary type memory. Usually they'll begin talking about it or like I said, if a memory comes up in a session, then I'll kind of tell them that there's a possibility that they may experience this**" (selective reinforcement; situational demands).

Subject #34:

Could you describe the concept of body memories?

"**Yes, if the feelings match the physical body memories, then we go looking for them, but I don't do it, they do it**" (traumatic reframing; survivor logic).

Does the concept of body memories correspond to the concept of cellular memories?

"I'm not sure what cellular memories . . . I don't know what you mean by cellular memories, so I don't know how to answer that question. Like in an NLP (neurolinguistic programming) form?"

Not necessarily, that seems to be entirely individual, everybody seems to have a different idea. Could you describe body memories a little more? Like how memories are stored in the body?

"Well, body memories that I thought we were talking about is when a client describes having either heavy pressure in a particular part of the body along with a feeling of shame or a feeling of excitement or a feeling of tremendous terror and for me, they don't work unless they come together. In other words, if somebody comes in and says, 'Well, I'm just experiencing a lot of vaginal pain,' then I say, 'Well, how does that feel?' and 'Well, I'm just experiencing a lot of pain,' then I say, 'Well, do you have any emotions around it?' 'No, I don't.' Then, I just let it go and think it's probably more about them looking for something than it is about what's going on."

Could you explain how memories are stored in the body?

"No."

Approximately what percentage of your clients experience body memories?

"Not that many. I don't know how to answer that either."

How can you tell when a client is experiencing a body memory?

"It seems to be unexpected. It seems to be, comes on when they're talking about something specific that has something to do with it. They may be talking about an older brother that they've always felt 'icky' around and then they might start experiencing some pain. They might start flopping around on the floor. They might start yelling and screaming. They might actually go into a spontaneous regression and remember the act (inadvertent hypnosis). You know, there's lots of different things. I guess I'm extremely cautious with this and I don't go looking for those things. They have to present them to me."

Subject #35:
Could you describe the concept of body memories?
"A body memory is a memory without cognitive aware-

ness of its origin or ideology. It's consistent with some type of trauma where a person may have been forced in a variety of ways and physically held, pushed or subjected to some external physical coercion, such as a memory of someone's, a feeling like someone's hands are around her throat, or a sensation like something cylindrical as in her vagina, or severe lower abdominal pain, or low back pain which later becomes a memory of the person's father lying with his erect penis against her low back and those types of things" (#2 and #3—somatic memory and memory stigmata theory; traumatic reframing).

Could you tell me anything about how the body stores memories?

"In terms of physiologically, I do not know how it happens but I think just like our brain stores memories of virtually everything that's happened to us and much that we've repressed, but are able to sometimes retrieve under appropriate situations (survivor logic). I think in the same way, apparently, the body has the ability to recall certain physical feelings and I do not know how that works. It seems to be a valid phenomena and is often triggered by certain events in the present that remind the person of some abusive thing from the past."

Does the concept of body memories correspond to the concept of cellular memories?

"I have heard it said that, yes, I mean to a degree it does, that our body, our cells, remember what has happened to us and then some things that happened are remembered at a cellular level. It's a phrase that's used. In terms of, in medical, physiological explanation, I couldn't give you one."

Approximately what percentage of your clients experience body memories?

"Of my total clientele or of the ones . . ."

How about both?

"Oh, boy, that's a little difficult to say. I would say that probably 80 to 100 percent of the ones who have definite memories of sexual abuse also have body memories. And of those who aren't sure, oh boy, it's just a wild guess, 50 percent or so of people who think they've, you know, have not totally ruled out the possibility of abuse but are wondering ought to have some type of body memory (attentional bias). Maybe it's higher than 50 percent. And of other people who I simply see, you know, I haven't paid as much attention to them, therefore they don't ask about it as often, so I really couldn't give any figures on that" (selective reinforcement; selective attention).

Okay, so it's not then as prevalent among clients who don't have a presenting problem or a suspected problem of sexual abuse?

"Right. It does not seem to be as prevalent. Some of that may be that my suspicion isn't as high and so I don't ask about it is all" (selective reinforcement; attentional bias).

How can you tell when a client is experiencing a body memory?

"I can't tell, but the client can tell. It's clearly subjective."

Subject #36:

Could you describe the concept of body memories?

"That a person will have, for example, feelings in their general area that indicate that their body is remembering something that happened to them earlier in their lives" (#6—mumbo jumbo).

Does the concept of body memories correspond to the concept of cellular memories?

"Yes."

Could you explain that a little more?

"Well, from what I understand, anything that happens in childhood that was not adequately resolved at the time gets stored on a cellular level and then is released when the person is either, well may be released when the person is ready for it or may be released at other times when there are triggers that access that cellular memory" (#2—sensory memory trigger theory; the "safe to remember" theory).

Approximately what percentage of your clients experience body memories?

"Maybe 40 percent."

How can you tell when a client is experiencing a body memory?

"I cannot necessarily tell unless they tell me."

Subject #37:

Could you describe the concept of body memories?

"To me, body memories might be something along the line of somebody watching a TV program and they have a certain amount of sensation, maybe pain and aching in the vaginal area and can't seem to figure out why during this particular program they're having this particular sensation and this comes up around certain themes, maybe around themes of violence, maybe around certain themes of aggression, maybe around children, living with children (#5—logical fallacy). So the concept of a body memory is like the body talking and a lot of times I believe that happens because certain abuse may have taken place before a child is verbal. So we hold the memory in an alternative form which is in the body."

Does the concept of body memories correspond to the concept of cellular memories?

"I don't know that I understand what cellular memory is exactly. It's a little more new to me, and my understanding of it is unclear, so I guess I don't use the two because I don't understand cellular memory."

Approximately what percentage of your clients experience body memories?

"I would say probably around 50 percent, maybe a little more than half."

How can you tell when a client is experiencing a body memory?

"Report, self-report. Sometimes witnessing while I'm with them, different kinds of tremors and ticks, pain, grabbing a shoulder or arm repeatedly after certain discussions, talking about coming through in terms of flashback which is self-report" (traumatic reframing).

Subject #38:

Could you describe the concept of body memories?

"Some sort of physiological sensation that is often times emotionally overwhelming, that the client can't relay, uh, or is confused about. There's no explanation why they have a burning sensation or a stabbing pain in their genital area or something along those lines that appears to be a body memory, where their body is remembering something that their mind has repressed" (# 5—logical fallacy).

Could you explain how the body stores memories?

"My theory?"

Yes.

"I believe that if someone is young enough and they don't really have the language to communicate what's happened, I believe the body remembers and people don't always remember with visual memories, but I believe that the body—actually, I believe all of us, with all of us our bodies take in what's happening to us throughout the day, through stress or through emotional pain. I believe there's a real connection between emotions and physiological symptoms"(#6—mumbo jumbo).

Does the concept of body memories correspond to the concept of cellular memories?

"I don't know."

Approximately what percentage of your clients experience body memories?

"What percentage of my clients that have been sexually abused?"

How about both? The general client load and then sexual abuse clients.

"About 25 percent, I guess I'd say."

Okay, of the regular client load?

"Well, regular client load if they haven't been sexually abused, I wouldn't know if they are body memories or they are actually, I've had people have like carry symptoms like if somebody's husband had a heart attack, all of a sudden she has chest pains, but I don't think that's about memory. I think that's about something else."

So then in general, if someone hasn't been sexually abused, they probably don't manifest body memories?

"Or, they don't talk about it if they do."

How can you tell when a client is experiencing a body memory?

"Usually, well a lot of them will dissociate (inadvertent hypnosis). **I mean, you can see kind of a shift, or a change, or they stop talking mid-stream and maybe they get flushed, or I've had some get really scared or start crying. Yes, usually, often times people will get really silent, like what's going on here? And I'll ask, you know, 'What's happening?' And sometimes they'll be like, 'I don't know what's happening, but I'm having this pain.' And then we'll work with that"** (traumatic reframing).

Conclusions

Although most of the therapists were careful to say that clients "self-reported" body memories, there were many indications that clients had to learn about body memories or have their so-called symptoms explained to them in survivor psychology terms by the therapists. Since the notion of body memories is currently unique to the recovery/survivor culture and a few eccentric mental and emotional health systems, clients had to find out about body memories in their therapeutic "journey." The vehicles are most likely to be either through the literature, the therapists, survivor groups and popular media. Another point that came up several times was that clients without sexual abuse memories or repressed memories were less likely to have body memories.

According to Lynn Gondolf, one of the first "retractors" of repressed memories to go public, the notion that all health problems were directly caused by sexual abuse and repressed memories was aggressively promoted in one clinic in which she had been an inpatient. Counselors in the clinic suggested that everything from breast cancer to the more common problems of simple yeast infections and urinary tract infections were caused by sexual abuse trauma. Simple medical problems were frequently related to "repressed" abuse issues. It appears that mental health practitioners are routinely overstepping their areas of expertise and are infringing on the territory of the medical profession. It is neither ethical nor wise to teach clients that medical problems have a direct cause and effect relationship to "repressed abuse" memories or that they are not actually medical problems but "body memories."

One therapist explained how she set up the process of traumatic thinking and traumatic reframing by explaining what she did to shape clients' expectancies and physical symptoms. Subject #33 said, "The most frequent time the issue of body memories comes up is when somebody is verging on remembering or believing that they're remembering. . . . Then their body might start remembering what happened to them and I'll give them some partial symptoms, some probabilities and usually at the point at which I'm doing that they look very relieved because it's already started. . . . And I tell them 'You know, I'm not telling you not to go to the doctor, but just be aware that this is very normal and to give it a little bit of time before you decide that something's wrong.' " When therapists advise clients to delay medical attention, it could be dangerous and potentially deadly. A lot of very common diseases or medical conditions could be occurring in conjunction with therapy and the so-called symptoms of these conditions could easily fit the descriptions of "body memories."

In the clinic where Gondolf first experienced false memories, she recalls that it was stated that every medical and emotional problem manifested by the clients in an eating disorder clinic could be cured by "remembering" the traumatic incident that was causing the memory.

One of the most common comments the therapists in my survey made were that the client reported unexplainable sensations that "were not connected to anything in the present."

Perhaps the best explanation of the concept of "cellular memories," (which along with body memories would be misnomers if this explanation were used and accepted by the therapeutic community), was from Subject #29 describing them as "all the defensive patterns that we've developed to deal with our emotional, or physical, or psychological abuse or neglect."

There are currently many types of deep muscle work that are based on similar theories, using less drastic techniques. However, the theory of muscular "armoring" and posturing as both emotional and physiological defense mechanisms makes sense for the manner in which they have been used by physical therapists. The body does adapt to physical and emotional stresses, and muscular formation and posture is related to these adaptations. But working on correcting misalignments in the body are far more conservative applications than using techniques with the intention of digging up memories.

The Scope of the Problem

The scientifically illiterate notions, revealed by the therapists in my survey, of how the mind, memory, brain and body work certainly should not be acceptable on the university level or within the mental health profession. If my survey results are indicative of how sexual abuse counselors conceptualize, talk about and teach about these notions, remedial education should be an immediate concern for practicing counselors and more science, ethics, physiological psychology, mental health history, social history and philosophy should be included in counseling and psychology programs.

The lack of understanding about the nature of suggestibility among the therapists interviewed was shocking. The subjective means of interpreting the presence of "repressed" sexual abuse memories by observing so-called "symptoms" has a very low chance of being even remotely accurate. Clients exposed to survivor psychology notions and therapists with attentional biases and biased interpretations of clients' feelings, experiences, dreams and so on, can create a cycle of social proof. Under these conditions, few clients could escape the repressed memory diagnosis.

It is astounding that so many therapists and self-appointed "child abuse" specialists are systematically denying that authority figures can profoundly influence clients and children, even if this influence is not intentional. Therapists are repeatedly cautioned about using clients to serve their own needs, beliefs and agendas. It is imperative that mental health professionals curb such tendencies, as well as remain aware and respectful of the client's condition and personality propensities such as fantasy-proneness, high suggestibility, high hypnotizability, histrionic tendencies, excessive emotional neediness, attention-seeking behaviors, and the tendency to want to please, conform or perform to perceived situational demands. What is most clearly indicated in the data from the Phoenix survey, and in reviewing the survivor manifestoes, is that the primary and ongoing educational processes for counselors and psychotherapists are failing in critical thinking, ethics, and biological, physiological and social psychology.

In defense of the survey participants, including the counselor who taught the initial seminar on counseling sexual abuse survivors, most would be appalled if they were able to see that their biases and invasive therapies contributed to their clients' misery and the destruction of relatively healthy and intact families. Hopefully, cognitive biases will not prevent them from facing the facts. It will take tremendous courage and integrity for counselors to abandon these treatment ideologies and modalities, and admit that they have been taken in by an ideology that became popular simply through repetition and overexposure.

National health care reform will certainly present a challenge to the practices and procedures of mental health professionals, but the greatest challenge comes from within the profession and from citizens. Are the majority of mental health professionals merely going to rearrange their prejudices, tailor their diagnoses to suit new policies and continue covertly practicing survivor psychology? Are therapists going to continue to think with their fears, hopes and wishes, and encourage clients to engage in this self-deception? Promoters of social pathology and garden variety psychological deviance seem compelled to twist all alternative viewpoints and evidence contrary to their ideology into an evil plot against women, children and God. Amid the tide of rumors, myths, urban legends and the abundant opinions of promoters of social deviance will hopefully spring a more rational view of social history and a far less pessimistic view of human nature.

APPENDIX

Profile of therapists who participated in the survey:

Subject	Age	M/F	Title	Years in Field	Academic Degree
1.	43	F	Creative Counselor	20	MSW
2.	NA	F	Psychotherapist	15	BA
3.	48	F	Counselor	16	BA
4.	48	F	Social worker	13	MSW
5.	48	F	Crisis Intervention Supervisor	6	BA
6.	33	F	Psychotherapist	6	MA
7.	32	F	Counselor	6	MAC
8.	47	F	Therapist	4	MAC
9.	NA	F	Counselor	8	MAC
10.	48	F	Cert. Clinical Therapist	NA	MAC
11.	57	F	Holistic Counselor	30	MA
12.	31	F	Therapist	3	BA
13.	54	M	Psychotherapist	27	PhD
14.	44	M	NA	20	PhD
15.	48	F	Psychotherapist	27	PhD
16.	37	F	Therapist	12	MSW
17.	49	F	Psychotherapist	8	MA

Subject	Age	M/F	Title	Years in Field	Academic Degree
18.	41	F	Psychotherapist	13	MAC
19.	25	F	Psychotherapist	5	MSW
20.	35	F	Therapist	5	MA
21.	31	F	Cert. Addiction Counselor	13	BS
22.	33	M	Psychotherapist	9	MAC
23.	49	F	Ind. Family Social Worker	7	MSW
24	37	F	Therapist	20	MA
25	63	F	Psychotherapist	8	MA
26.	35	F	Psychotherapist	4	MAC
27.	47	F	Cert. Professional Counselor	10	BA
28.	39	M	Clinical Assistant	4	BA
29.	39	M	Psychologist	13	PhD
30.	50	F	Marriage&Family Therapist	12	BA
31.	45	F	Therapist	10	MAC
32.	37	M	Cert. Ind. Social Worker	15	None
33.	37	F	Psychotherapist	8	MA
34.	52	F	Psychotherapist	13	MAC
35.	45	M	Psychotherapist	6	MAC
36.	47	F	Psychotherapist	13	MAC
37.	42	F	Psychotherapist, Consultant	20	MAC
38.	34	F	Cert. Ind. Social Worker	NA	MSW

Partial results from the survey of 38 therapists from the Phoenix area:

Can you identify a client with repressed sexual abuse issues before the client identifies the problem?
Sometimes 29%
Yes 71%

Do you suggest the possibility of repressed sexual abuse issues in a client?
Sometimes 66%
Yes 17%
No 17%

Do you affirm the client's tentative impressions, dreams or feelings that may indicate sexual abuse?
Sometimes 28%
Yes 66%
No 6%

Do you validate the possibility that sexual abuse occurred and that traumatic memories are often repressed?
Sometimes 17%
Yes 83%

Do you use a sexual abuse and incest survivor checklist to diagnose repressed abuse?
Sometimes 17%
Yes 32%
No 51%

Is it of any importance to the therapeutic process whether recovered memories are true or false?
Yes 34%
No 76%

Have you encountered clients with sexual abuse issues who have Post Traumatic Stress Disorder?

> **Yes** **69%**
> **No** **31%**

Have you encountered clients with sexual abuse issues who have Multiple Personality Disorder?

> **Yes** **89%**
> **No** **11%**

Have you encountered clients reporting satanic abuse?

> **Yes** **92%**
> **No** **8%**

Have you attended seminars or training sessions on satanic abuse?

> **Yes** **70%**
> **No** **30%**

Do you consider ritual and satanic abuse to be serious problems in the sexual abuse field?

> **Yes** **97%**

Do you use any of the following techniques to uncover or clarify memories?

Hypnosis .... Yes—63%

Trance work .... Yes—71%

Age regression .... Yes—79%

Non-dominant handwriting .... Yes—76%

Dream interpretation .... Yes—89%

Psychodrama .... Yes—63%

Art therapy .... Yes—71%

Assign or make available survivor
books such as *The Courage to Heal*
and S*ecret Survivors* .... Yes—100%

Which of the syndromes and disorders are commonly symptoms of sexual abuse, incest and repressed abuse issues?

Alcoholism .... Yes—97%

Drug addiction .... Yes—95%

Eating disorders .... Yes—97%

Depression .... Yes—97%

Sexual dysfunction .... Yes—97%

Sexual addiction .... Yes—97%

Relationship addiction .... Yes—95%

Health problems .... Yes—95%

Cancer... Yes—71%

MPD .... Yes—95%

PTSD .... Yes—92%

Dissociative disorders .... Yes—92%

Childhood amnesia .... Yes—71%

Gynecological problems .... Yes—97%

Is it common for memories to surface in the following ways?

Dreams .... Yes—95%

Flashbacks .... Yes—95%

Body memories .... Yes—95%

Hypnosis or trance work .... Yes—95%

During survivor groups .... Yes—95%

Anniversaries of abuse .... Yes—95%

Sensory memory triggers................... Yes—87%

TV programs with sexual
abuse themes .... Yes—68%

NOTES

CHAPTER ONE

Page 6   *These programs have adopted:* "Results of the FMSF Family Survey," by P. Freyd, Z. Roth, H. Wakefield and R. Underwager (1993, FMS Foundation).

     7   *The notion is not new:* See *Fads and Fallacies in the Name of Science,* by Martin Gardner (1957, Dover Publications).

     7   *Some adults suffer:* See *The Child Abuse Industry,* by Mary Pride (1986, Crossway Books).

   11   *The new ideology of:* See *The Courage to Heal,* by Ellen Bass and Laura Davis (1988, Harper & Row).

CHAPTER TWO

Page 17   *The Canadian orphans:* ABC News *PrimeTime Live,* May 6, 1993.

   18   *Various medicinal:* See *The Food of the Gods,* by Terence McKenna (1992, Bantam Books).

   19   *In the early 1900s:* See *The Way We Never Were,* by Stephanie Coontz (1992, Basic Books).

   20   *Social psychologist Richard Ofshe:* "Inadvertent Hypnosis During Interrogation: False Confession Due to Dissociative State, Misidentified Multiple Personality and the Satanic Cult Hypothesis," by Richard Ofshe, *The International Journal of Clinical and Experimental Hypnosis* (1992).

   20   *Survivor and recovery psychologists:* See *Satan's Children,* by Robert S. Mayer (1991, Avon Books);

Repressed Memories, by Renee Fredrickson (1992, Simon & Schuster); *Bradshaw On: The Family,* by John Bradshaw (1987, Health Communications).

21 *Subsidy programs:* See *The Way We Never Were,* by Stephanie Coontz.

21 *The shift from diagnostic:* See *The Shrinking of America: The Myth of Psychological Change,* by Bernie Zilbergeld (1983, Little Brown).

22 *Confessional orgies:* See *Bradshaw On: The Family,* by John Bradshaw; *Healing the Shame that Binds You,* by John Bradshaw (1988, Health Communications); *Homecoming,* by John Bradshaw (1990, Bantam Books); *Secret Survivors,* by E. Sue Blume (1990, Ballantine Books).

CHAPTER THREE

Page 27 *In 1992 I completed:* "Inquiry into Current Sexual Abuse Treatment Modalities," by Susan Smith (1992, Ottawa University, Phoenix, AZ).

28 *The term persuasion:* See *Age of Propaganda: The Everyday Use and Abuse of Persuasion,* by Anthony Pratkanis and Elliot Aronson (1991, W. H. Freeman and Company).

35 *Until the early 1980s there were:* See *Magic, Mischief and Memories,* by Hollida Wakefield and Ralph Underwager (1991, Institute for Psychological Therapies).

36 *The idea is that "if dependency needs:* See *Bradshaw On: The Family,* by John Bradshaw.

36 *If the client reports "funny looks":* See *Secret Survivors,* by E. Sue Blume.

38 *This is not consistent with the flashback:* See *The Sex Abuse Hysteria,* by Richard Gardner (1991, Creative Therapeutics).

39 *Sometimes these experiences are believed to be:* See *The Courage to Heal,* by Ellen Bass and Laura Davis; *Repressed Memories,* by Renee Fredrickson.

42 *In 1778, Anton Mesmer:* See *Abnormal Psychology and*

Modern Life, by Robert Carson, James Butcher and James Coleman (1988, Scott, Foresman).

43 *Infant amnesia is a naturally:* See *Suggestions of Abuse,* by Michael Yapko (1994, Simon & Schuster).

43 *We do alter our memories:* "A Case of Misplaced Nostalgia," by Ulric Neisser, *American Psychologist* (1991).

50 *Two-thirds of the normal:* See *Comprehensive Textbook of Psychiatry,* by Harold Kaplan and Benjamin Sadock (1985, Williams and Wilkins).

52 *In its extreme form it is:* See *Patient or Pretender: Inside the Strange World of Factitious Disorders,* by Marc Feldman and Charles Ford (1994, John Wiley and Sons).

53 *The majority of patients diagnosed:* See *Magic, Mischief and Memories,* by Hollida Wakefield and Ralph Underwager.

CHAPTER FOUR

Page 61 *Sociologists have traced:* See *Satanic Panic: The Creation of a Contemporary Legend,* by Jeffrey Victor (1993, Open Court).

61 *Although urban legends:* See *Abnormal Psychology and Modern Life,* by Robert Carson, James Butcher and James Coleman.

61 *As more professionals develop:* See *In Pursuit of Satan: The Police and the Occult,* by Robert Hicks (1991, Prometheus Books).

61 *This contagion trend:* See *Abnormal Psychology and Modern Life,* by Robert Carson, James Butcher and James Coleman.

62 *The dance mania:* See *Abnormal Psychology and Modern Life,* by Robert Carson, James Butcher and James Coleman.

62 *The illnesses were initially:* "Satanic Cult 'Survivor' Stories," by Jeffrey Victor, *Skeptical Inquirer* (Spring 1992).

62 *Writer Jem Sullivan Says:* "Psychiatrists: Help the Ab-

ducted," by Jem Sullivan, *New Age Journal* (October 1992).

63   *Laibow began looking:* "Dark Side of the Unknown," by Patrick Huyghe, *Omni* (September 1993).

63   *Therapists who become:* "Dark Side of the Unknown," by Patrick Huyghe.

64   *Criteria do exist:* "Recovered Memories of Alleged Sexual Abuse: Lawsuits Against Parents," by Hollida Wakefield and Ralph Underwager, *Behavioral Sciences and the Law* (in press); *Suggestions of Abuse,* by Michael Yapko (1994, Simon & Schuster).

64   *The practice of reporting hunches:* See *The Sex Abuse Hysteria,* by Richard Gardner.

66   *Bulimia may be present:* "Treating the Diseases of the 1980s: Eating Disorders," by J. P. Foreyt, *Contemporary Psychology* (1986).

68   *Factoid manifestoes can be identified:* See *Age of Propaganda,* by Anthony Pratkanis and Elliot Aronson.

70   *Hovland's learning model of influence:* See *Age of Propaganda,* by Anthony Pratkanis and Elliot Aronson.

75   *It has been well known among social psychologists:* See *Age of Propaganda,* by Anthony Pratkanis and Elliot Aronson; *The Rape of the Mind,* by Joost Meerloo (1961, Grosset and Dunlap).

76   *George Orwell, author of the:* See *Writing that Works,* by Richard Andersen (1989, McGraw-Hill).

76   *In his forbidden diary:* See *1984,* by George Orwell (1949, New American Library).

80   *After researching the field of UFOlogy:* "Dark Side of the Unknown," by Patrick Huyghe.

85   *Now we have performing MPDs:* "Truddi Chase, Multiple Personalities," *Oprah Winfrey Show* (August 4, 1993).

86   *The hypnotic model of persuasion:* See *Professional Hypnotism Manual,* by John Kappas (1987, Panorama).

87   *On the other hand, the notion:* See *They Call It Hypnosis,* by Robert Baker (1990, Prometheus Books).

88 *This scrambles the usual defense:* See *Professional Hypnotism Manual,* by John Kappas.

88 *This is why simple relaxation:* "Making Monsters," by Richard Ofshe and Ethan Watters, *Society* (March/April 1993).

93 *However, there is nothing scientific:* See *Psychological Testing,* by Anne Anastasi (1988, Macmillan).

94 *The laundry list describes:* See *The Laundry List: The ACOA Experience,* by Tony A. and Dan F. (1991, Health Communications).

94 *In one such study, Sher and Logue:* See *Children of Alcoholics: A Critical Appraisal of Theory and Research,* by Kenneth Sher (1991, University of Chicago Press).

96 *Many recovery culture and therapeutic:* See *Co-Dependence: Misunderstood, Mistreated,* by Anne Wilson Schaef (1986, Harper & Row); *When Society Becomes an Addict,* by Anne Wilson Schaef (1987, Harper & Row).

CHAPTER FIVE

Page 103 *Two main organizing principles:* See *Bradshaw On: The Family,* by John Bradshaw; *Healing the Shame that Binds You,* by John Bradshaw (1988, Health Communications).

105 *Literally manifesting:* See *Homecoming,* by John Bradshaw (1990, Bantam Books).

111 *For instance, the term abandonment:* See *Bradshaw On: The Family,* by John Bradshaw.

111 *The word "addiction" describes:* See *When Society Becomes an Addict,* by Anne Wilson Schaef.

115 *It is hard enough to accept:* Personal communication with Jan Hansen (1993).

119 *Teenagers are known for:* See *Satanic Panic,* by Jeffrey Victor.

123 *It is claimed that men remain:* See *Lessons in Evil, Lessons from the Light,* by Gail Feldman (1993, Crown).

125 *Among academically and scientifically:* See *Abnormal*

Psychology and Modern Life, by Robert Carson, James Butcher and James Coleman.

CHAPTER SIX

Page 135   *Although the majority of highly hypnotizable:* See *Comprehensive Textbook of Psychiatry,* by Harold Kaplan and Benjamin Sadock.

    156   *The mass madness and abnormal behavior:* See *Abnormal Psychology and Modern Life,* by Robert Carson, James Butcher and James Coleman.

BIBLIOGRAPHY

A., Tony and F., Dan (1991). *The Laundry List: The ACOA Experience.* Deerfield Beach, FL: Health Communications.

Ackerman, Robert (1989). *Perfect Daughters: Adult Daughters of Alcoholics.* Deerfield Beach, FL: Health Communications.

Alcoholics Anonymous (3rd ed.) (1976). New York: Alcoholics Anonymous World Services.

Alcoholics Anonymous Comes of Age: A Brief History of A.A. (12th ed.) (1986). New York: Alcoholics Anonymous World Services.

American Psychiatric Association (1987). *Diagnostic and Statistical Manual of Mental Disorders, Third Edition—Revised.* Washington, D.C: American Psychiatric Association.

Anastasi, Anne (1988). *Psychological Testing* (6th ed.). New York: MacMillan.

Andersen, Richard (1989). *Writing that Works.* New York: McGraw-Hill.

Baker, Robert A. (1990). *They Call It Hypnosis.* Buffalo, NY: Prometheus Books.

_____ (1992). *Hidden Memories.* Buffalo, NY: Prometheus Books.

Balis, Susan (1989). *Beyond the Illusion: Choices for Children of Alcoholics.* Deerfield Beach, FL: Health Communications.

Barker, Sandra B. and Bitter, James Robert (1992). "Early Recollections Versus Created Memory: A Comparison for Projective Qualities." *Individual Psychology, 48* (1), 87.

Baron, Robert A. and Byrne, Donn Erwin (1991). *Social Psychology: Understanding Human Interaction* (6th ed.). Boston: Allyn and Bacon.

Basil, Robert (Ed.) (1988). *Not Necessarily the New Age.* Buffalo, NY: Prometheus Books.

Bass, Ellen and Davis, Laura (1988). *The Courage to Heal*. New York: Harper & Row.

Beattie, Melody (1987). *Codependent No More*. Center City, MN: Hazelden.

_____ (1989). *Beyond Co-Dependency*. New York: Harper & Row.

Becker, Robert A. (1989). *Addicted to Misery: The Other Side of Co-Dependency*. Deerfield Beach, FL: Health Communications.

Black, Claudia (1981). *It Will Never Happen to Me!* New York: Ballantine Books.

Blume, E. Sue (1990). *Secret Survivors: Uncovering Incest and Its Aftereffects in Women*. New York: Ballantine Books.

Boskind-White, M. and White, W. C. (1987). *Bulimarexia: The Binge/Purge Cycle*. New York: W. W. Norton.

Bradshaw, John (1987). *Bradshaw On: The Family*. Deerfield Beach, FL: Health Communications.

_____ (1988). *Healing the Shame that Binds You*. Deerfield Beach, FL: Health Communications.

_____ (1990). *Homecoming*. New York: Bantam Books.

Brown, Stephanie; Beletsis, Susan; and Cermak, Timmen (1989). *Adult Children of Alcoholics in Treatment*. Deerfield Beach, FL: Health Communications.

Buchanan, Linda Paulk; Kern, Roy; and Bell-Dumas, Jean (1991). "Comparison of Content in Created Versus Actual Early Recollections." *Individual Psychology*, 47 (3), 348-355.

Bufe, Charles (1991). *Alcoholics Anonymous: Cult or Cure?* San Francisco: Sharp Press.

Carson, Robert C.; Butcher, James N.; and Coleman, James C. (1988). *Abnormal Psychology and Modern Life* (8th ed.). Glenview, IL: Scott, Foresman.

Chaplin, James P. (1985). *Dictionary of Psychology* (2nd ed.). New York: Laurel Books.

Chase, Truddi (1987). *When Rabbit Howls*. New York: Jove.

Christopher, James (1988). *How to Stay Sober: Recovery Without Religion*. Buffalo, NY: Prometheus Books.

_____ (1992). *SOS Sobriety: The Proven Alternative to the 12 Steps*. Buffalo NY: Prometheus Books.

Cialdini, Robert (1984). *Influence: How and Why People Agree to Things*. New York: Morrow.

Cooney, Timothy J. (1991). *The Difference Between Truth and Opinion: How the Misuse of Language Can Lead to Disaster*. Buffalo,

NY: Prometheus Books.

Coontz, Stephanie (1992). *The Way We Never Were: American Families and the Nostalgia Trap.* New York: Basic Books.

Corey, Gerald (1991). *Theory and Practice of Counseling and Psychotherapy.* Monterey, CA: Brooks/Cole.

Covitz, Joel (1986). *Emotional Child Abuse.* Boston: Sigo Press.

Cruse, Joseph R. (1989). *Painful Affairs: Looking for Love Through Addiction and Co-Dependency.* Deerfield Beach, FL: Health Communications.

Daly, Laurence W. and Pacifico, J. Frank (1991, December). "Opening the Doors to the Past: Decade Delayed Disclosure of Memories of Years Gone By." *The Champion.*

Dawes, Robyn (1991). "Biases of Retrospection." *Issues in Child Abuse Accusations, 1* (3), 25-28.

Doe, Jane (1991). "How Could This Happen? Coping with a False Accusation of Incest and Rape." *Issues in Child Abuse Accusations, 3* (3), 154-165.

Dowd, Maureen (1989, October). "Addiction Chic: Are We Hooked on Being Hooked?" *Mademoiselle,* 216-217.

Duncan, C. W. (1993, October). "The Truth About MPD." *Changes,* 79-84.

Eberle, Paul and Shirley (1993). *The Abuse of Innocence: The McMartin Preschool Trial.* Buffalo, NY: Prometheus Books.

Feldman, Gail (1993). *Lessons in Evil, Lessons from the Light.* New York: Crown.

Femina, Donna Della; Yeager, Catherine A.; and Lewis, Dorothy Otnow (1990). "Child Abuse: Adolescent Records vs Adult Recall." *Child Abuse and Neglect, 14,* 227-231.

Foreyt, J. P. (1986). "Treating the Diseases of the 1980s: Eating Disorders." *Contemporary Psychology, 31,* 658-660.

Fossum, Merle A. and Mason, Marilyn J. (1986). *Facing Shame: Families in Recovery.* New York: W. W. Norton.

Fredrickson, Renee (1992). *Repressed Memories: A Journey to Recovery from Sexual Abuse.* New York: Simon & Schuster.

French, Christopher; Fowler, Mandy; McCarthy, Katy; and Peers, Debbie (1990, Winter). "Belief in Astrology: A Test of the Barnum Effect." *Skeptical Inquirer, 15* (2).

Friedman, William J. (1991). "The Development of Children's Memory for the Time of Past Events." *Child Development, 62,* 139-155.

Friesen, James G. (1991). *Uncovering the Mystery of MPD: Its Shock-*

ing Origins, Its Surprising Cure. San Bernardino, CA: Here's Life Publishers.

Ganaway, George (1991, August 19). "Alternative Hypotheses Regarding Satanic Ritual Abuse Memories." Paper presented at the 99th Annual Convention of the American Psychological Association, San Francisco, CA.

Gardner, Martin (1957). *Fads and Fallacies in the Name of Science.* New York: Dover Publications.

Gardner, Richard (1991). *The Sex Abuse Hysteria: Salem Witch Trials Revisited.* Cresskill, NJ: Creative Therapeutics.

_____ (1992). *True and False Accusations of Child Sex Abuse.* Cresskill, NJ: Creative Therapeutics.

_____ (1993, February 22). "Modern Witch Hunt—Child Abuse Charges." *The Wall Street Journal.*

Garland, R. J. and Doughter, M. J. (1990). "The Abused/Abuser Hypothesis of Child Sexual Abuse: A Critical Review of Theory and Research." In J. R. Feierman (Ed.), *Pedophilia: Biosocial Dimensions.* New York: Springer-Verlag.

Glaser, Danya and Collins, Carole (1988). "The Response of Young, Non-Sexually Abused Children to Anatomically Correct Dolls." *Journal of Child Psychology and Psychiatry, 30,* 547-560.

Goldberg, Steven (1991). *When Wish Replaces Thought: Why So Much of What You Believe Is False.* Buffalo, NY: Prometheus Books.

Goldstein, Eleanor (1992). *Confabulations.* Boca Raton, FL: SIRS Books.

Goldstein, Eleanor and Farmer, Kevin (1993). *True Stories of False Memories.* Boca Raton, FL: SIRS Books.

Goleman, Daniel (1992, July 21). "Childhood Trauma: Memory or Invention?" *New York Times.*

_____ (1993, April 6). "Studying the Secrets of Childhood Memory." *New York Times.*

Goodman, Gail S. (1984). "The Child Witness: An Introduction." *Journal of Social Issues, 40* (2), 1-7.

_____ (1984). "Children's Testimony in Historical Perspective." *Journal of Social Issues, 40* (2), 9-31.

_____ (1990). "Children's Use of Anatomically Detailed Dolls to Recount an Event." *Child Development, 61* (6) 1859-1871.

Gregg, V. H. (1987). "Hypnotic Pseudomemory: Continuing Issues." *British Journal of Experimental and Clinical Hypnosis, 4,* 109-111.

Hay, Louise (1988). *Heal Your Body*. Santa Monica, CA: Hay House.

Heiman, Marsha L. (1992). "Annotation: Putting the Puzzle Together: Validating Allegations of Child Sexual Abuse." *Journal of Child Psychiatry, 33* (2), 311-329.

Helfer, Ray E. (1991). "Child Abuse and Neglect: Assessment, Treatment, and Prevention." *Journal of Child Psychiatry, 15* (1), 5-15.

Hicks, Robert (1991). *In Pursuit of Satan: The Police and the Occult.* Buffalo, NY: Prometheus Press.

Hillman, James and Ventura, Michael (1992, May/June). "Is Therapy Turning Us into Children?" *New Age Journal.*

_____ (1992). *We've Had a Hundred Years of Psychotherapy and the World's Getting Worse.* San Francisco: Harper San Francisco.

Hoorwitz, Aaron (1992). *The Clinical Detective.* New York: W. W. Norton.

Hubbard, L. Ron (1991). *Dianetics: The Modern Science of Mental Health.* Los Angeles: Bridge Publications.

Huyghe, Patrick. (1993, September). "Dark Side of the Unknown." *Omni.*

Jennings, Marianne Moody (1992, May 17). "Mommy Dearest Madness." *Arizona Republic.*

Jonker, F. and Jonker-Bakker, P. (1991). "Experiences with Ritualistic Child Abuse: A Case Study from the Netherlands." *Child Abuse and Neglect, 15,* 191-196.

Kaminer, Wendy (1992). *I'm Dysfunctional, You're Dysfunctional.* Reading, MA: Addison-Wesley.

Kaplan, Harold I. and Sadock, Benjamin J. (Eds.) (1985). *Comprehensive Textbook of Psychiatry* (4th ed.). Baltimore: Williams and Wilkins.

Kappas, John G. (1987). *Professional Hypnotism Manual* (2nd ed.). Van Nuys, CA: Panorama.

Kasl, Charlotte Davis. (1990, November/December). "The 12-Step Controversy." *Ms.*

Katz, Stan J. and Liu, Aimee (1991). *The Codependency Conspiracy.* New York: Warner Books.

Kritsberg, Wayne (1985). *The Adult Children of Alcoholics Syndrome.* Pompano Beach, FL: Health Communications.

Lanning, K. V. (1989, October). "Satanic, Occult, Ritualistic Crime: A Law Enforcement Perspective." *Police Chief, 56* (10), 62-72.

_____ (1991). "Ritual Abuse: A Law Enforcement View or Perspective." *Child Abuse and Neglect, 15* (3), 171-173.

_____(1992, January). "Investigator's Guide to Allegations of

'Ritual' Child Abuse." National Center for the Analysis of Violent Crime, FBI Academy.

Lee, John (1989). *The Flying Boy: Healing the Wounded Man.* Deerfield Beach, FL: Health Communications.

Lingg, Mary Ann and Kottham, Terry (1991). "Changing Mistaken Beliefs Through Visualizations of Early Recollections." *Individual Psychology, 47* (2), 255-260.

Loftus, Elizabeth, F. (1993). "The Reality of Repressed Memories." *American Psychologist, 48* (5), 518-37.

Lynn, Steven J. and Rhue, Judith W. (1988). "Fantasy Proneness: Hypnosis, Developmental Antecedents, and Psychopathology." *American Psychologist, 43* (1), 35-44.

Masson, Jeffrey Moussaieff (1984). *The Assault on Truth.* New York: HarperCollins.

Mayer, Robert A. (1988). *Through Divided Minds: Probing the Mysteries of Multiple Personalities—A Doctor's Story.* New York: Bantam Doubleday.

_____ (1991). *Satan's Children: Case Studies in Multiple Personality.* New York: Avon Books.

McKenna, Terence (1992). *Food of the Gods: A Radical History of Plants, Drugs and Human Evolution.* New York: Bantam Books.

Meacham, Andrew. (1993, April). "Presumed Guilty." *Changes.*

Meerloo, Joost (1961). *The Rape of the Mind: The Psychology of Thought Control, Menticide and Brainwashing.* New York: Grosset & Dunlap.

Miller, Alice (1984). *For Your Own Good: Hidden Cruelty in Child-Rearing and the Roots of Violence.* New York: Farrar, Straus & Giroux.

_____ (1984). *Thou Shalt Not Be Aware: Society's Betrayal of the Child.* New York: Farrar, Straus & Giroux.

_____ (1990). *The Untouched Key: Tracing Childhood Trauma in Creativity and Destructiveness.* New York: Anchor Books.

Miller, Michael Vincent (1992, May 17). "How We Suffer Now." *New York Times Book Review.*

Moorhead, M. V. (1992, February/March). "Is Acting Really in Your Blood?" *Phoenix New Times.*

Morris, Michael (1992, April 21). " 'False Memory Syndrome' Taking Its Toll on Families." *Utah County Journal.*

Mrazek, Patricia and Mrazek, David A. (1987). "Resilience in Child Maltreatment Victims: A Conceptual Exploration." *Child Abuse and Neglect, 11,* 357-366.

Muro, Mark (1992, April 14). "New Voices Declare Independence from Codependence." *Arizona Republic.*

Nakken, Craig (1988). *The Addictive Personality: Understanding Compulsion in Our Lives.* San Francisco: Harper & Row.

Neisser, Ulric (1991). "A Case of Misplaced Nostalgia." *American Psychologist,* 46 (1), 34-36.

Ofshe, Richard (1992). "Inadvertent Hypnosis During Interrogation: False Confessions Due to Dissociative State, Misidentified Multiple Personality and the Satanic Cult Hypothesis." *The International Journal of Clinical and Experimental Hypnosis, XL* (3), 125-156.

Ofshe, Richard and Watters, Ethan (1993, March/April). "Making Monsters." *Society.*

Orne, M. T.; Dinges, D. F.; and Orne, E. C. (1984). "On Differential Diagnosis of Multiple Personality in the Forensic Context." *International Journal of Clinical and Experimental Hypnosis, 32* (2), 118-169.

Orne, M. T.; Soskis, D. A.; Dinges, D. F.; Orne, E. C.; and Tonry, M. H. (1985). "Hypnotically Refreshed Testimony: Enhanced Memory or Tampering with Evidence?" U.S. Department of Justice, National Institute of Justice.

Orwell, George (1949). *1984.* New York: New American Library.

Paine-Gernee, Karen and Hunt, Terry (1990). *Emotional Healing: A Program for Emotional Sobriety.* New York: Warner Books.

Peck, Scott M. (1978). *The Road Less Traveled.* New York: Simon & Schuster.

_____ (1983). *People of the Lie.* New York: Simon & Schuster.

Peele, Stanton (1985). *The Meaning of Addiction.* Lexington, MA: D.C. Heath & Company.

_____ (1989). *Diseasing of America: Addiction Treatment Out of Control.* Lexington, MA: D. C. Heath & Company.

_____ (1991). *The Truth About Addiction and Recovery.* New York: Simon & Schuster.

Pope, Harrison G., Jr. and Hudson, James L. (1992). "Is Childhood Sexual Abuse a Risk Factor for Bulimia Nervosa?" *American Journal of Psychiatry, 149* (4), 455-463.

Pratkanis, Anthony and Aronson, Elliot (1991). *Age of Propaganda: The Everyday Use and Abuse of Persuasion.* New York: W. H. Freeman and Company.

Pride, Mary (1986). *The Child Abuse Industry.* Westchester, IL: Crossway Books.

Putnam, Frank W. (1991). "The Satanic Abuse Controversy." *Child Abuse and Neglect, 15,* 175-179.

Ragge, Ken (1991). *More Revealed: A Critical Analysis of Alcoholics Anonymous and the Twelve Steps.* Henderson, NV: Alert Publishing.

Richardson, J. T.; Best, J.; and Bromley, D. G. (Eds.) (1991). *The Satanism Scare.* New York: Aldine de Gruyter.

Robinson, E. J. and Mitchell, P. (1992). "Children's Interpretation of Messages from a Speaker with a False Belief." *Child Development, 63,* 639-652.

Schaef, Anne Wilson (1986). *Co-Dependence: Misunderstood, Mistreated.* San Francisco: Harper & Row.

_____ (1987). *When Society Becomes an Addict.* San Francisco: Harper & Row.

Schaef, Ann Wilson and Fassel, Diane (1988). *The Addictive Organization.* San Francisco: Harper & Row.

Schaeffer, Brenda (1987). "Is It Love, or Is It Addiction?" New York: Harper/Hazelden.

Sex and Love Addicts Anonymous (1986). Boston: Fellowship-Wide Services.

Sher, Kenneth (1991). *Children of Alcoholics: A Critical Appraisal of Theory and Research.* Chicago: University of Chicago Press.

Shore, Lys Ann (1991, Spring). "After the New Age: The Recovery Trend." *Skeptical Inquirer, 15* (3).

Smith, Michelle and Pazder, Lawrence (1980). *Michelle Remembers.* New York: Congdon and Lattes.

Smith, Susan E. (1986). *Fear or Freedom: A Woman's Options in Social Survival and Physical Defense.* Racine, WI: Mother Courage Press.

_____ (1992). "Essay by an Escapee from Recovery Cultism to an Empowerment System." In J. Christopher, *SOS Sobriety.* Buffalo, NY: Prometheus Books.

Spanos, N. P.; Bridgeman, M.; Stam, H. J.; Gwynn, M. I.; and Saad, C. I. (1983). "When Seeing Is Not Believing: The Effects of Contextual Variables on the Reports of Hypnotic Hallucinations." *Imagination, Cognition and Personality, 2,* 195-209.

Spanos, Nicholas P. and Chaves, John F. (Eds.) (1989). *Hypnosis: The Cognitive-Behavioral Perspective.* New York: Prometheus Books.

Statton, Jane Ellis and Wilborn, Bobbie (1991). "Adlerian Counseling and Early Recollections of Children." *Individual Psy-*

chology, 47 (1), 339-347.

Steele, Brandt F. (1986). "Notes on the Lasting Effects of Early Child Abuse Throughout the Life Cycle." *Child Abuse and Neglect, 10,* 283-291.

Steinem, Gloria (1992). *Revolution from Within: A Book of Self-Esteem.* Boston: Little, Brown.

Stewart, James R. (1991, Winter). "The West Bank Collective Hysteria Episode: The Politics of Illness." *Skeptical Inquirer, 15* (2).

Stratford, Lauren. (1988). *Satan's Underground: An Extraordinary Story of One Woman's Escape.* Gretna, LA: Pelican Publishing.

Striano, Judy (1988). *Can Psychotherapists Hurt You?* Santa Barbara, CA: Professional Press.

Strober, M. (1986). "Anorexia Nervosa: History and Psychological Concepts." In K. D. Brownell and J. P. Foreyt (Eds.), *Handbook of Eating Disorders.* New York: Basic Books.

Subby, Robert (1987). *Lost in the Shuffle: The Co-Dependent Reality.* Deerfield Beach, FL: Health Communications.

Sullivan, Jem (1992, October). "Psychiatrists: Help the Abducted." *New Age Journal.*

Szasz, Thomas (1983). *Primary Values and Major Contentions.* Buffalo, NY: Prometheus Books.

_____ (1984). *The Therapeutic State: Psychiatry in the Mirror of Current Events.* Buffalo, NY: Prometheus Books.

Tavris, Carol (1992). *The Mismeasure of Woman.* New York: Simon & Schuster.

_____ (1993, January 3). "Beware the Incest Survivor Machine." *New York Times Book Review.*

Taylor, Bill (1992, May 16, 18, 19). "What If Sexual Abuse Memories Are Wrong?" *Toronto Star.*

Taylor, Peggy (1992, September/October). "The Way We Never Were: Interview with Stephanie Coontz." *New Age Journal.*

Thiriart, Philippe (1991, Winter). "Acceptance of Personality Test Results." *Skeptical Inquirer, 15* (2).

Torrey, E. Fuller (1992). *Freudian Fraud.* New York: HarperCollins.

Toufexis, Anastasia. (1991, October 28). "When Can Memories Be Trusted?" *Time.*

Utain, Marsha and Oliver, Barbara (1989). *Scream Louder: Through Hell and Healing with an Incest Survivor and Her Therapist.* Deerfield Beach, FL: Health Communications.

Vanderbilt, Heidi (1992, February). "Incest: A Chilling Report." *Lears.*

Victor, Jeffrey (1992, Spring). "Satanic Cult 'Survivor' Stories." *Skeptical Inquirer, 15* (3).

_____ (1993). *Satanic Panic: The Creation of a Contemporary Legend*. Chicago and La Salle, IL: Open Court.

Wakefield, Hollida and Underwager, Ralph (1992). *Magic, Mischief, and Memories: Remembering Repressed Abuse*. Northfield, MN: Institute for Psychological Therapies.

_____ (1992). "Recovered Memories of Alleged Sexual Abuse: Lawsuits Against Parents." *Behavioral Sciences and the Law*, in press.

White, Marlene and White, William (1981, May). "Bingeing and Purging." *Glamour*.

Whitfield, Charles (1991). *Co-Dependence: Healing the Human Condition*. Deerfield Beach, FL: Health Communications.

Whitley, Glenna (1991, October). "The Seduction of Gloria Grady." *D Magazine*.

_____ (1992, January). "Abuse of Trust." *D Magazine*.

Widom, Cathy Spatz (1990, April). "The Cycle of Violence." *Science 14*, 160-165.

Wielawski, Irene (1991, October 3). "Unlocking the Secrets of Memory." *Los Angeles Times*.

Wilson, Bill (1967). *As Bill Sees It: The A A Way of Life*. New York: Alcoholics Anonymous World Services.

Woititz, Janet (1983). *Adult Children of Alcoholics*. Deerfield Beach, FL: Health Communications.

Yant, Martin (1991). *Presumed Guilty: When Innocent People Are Wrongly Convicted*. Buffalo, NY: Prometheus Books.

Yapko, Michael (1994). *Suggestions of Abuse*. New York: Simon & Schuster.

Young, Walter C.; Sachs, Roberta; Braun, Bennett G.; and Watkins, Ruth (1991). "Patients Reporting Ritual Abuse in Childhood: A Clinical Syndrome Report of 37 Cases." *Child Abuse and Neglect 15*, 181-189.

Zeig, Jeffrey K. (Ed.) (1987). *The Evolution of Psychotherapy*. New York: Brunner/Mazel.

Zilbergeld, Bernie (1983). *The Shrinking of America: Myths of Psychological Change*. Boston: Little, Brown.

Zweig, Connie and Abrams, Jeremiah (1991). *Meeting the Shadow: The Hidden Power of the Dark Side of Human Nature*. Los Angeles: Jeremy P. Tarcher, Inc.

INDEX

DATE DUE

DEMCO